Chifley and Australian Postwar Reconstruction: the Australian Labor Party and the Federal Platform 1945-1949

Dr John McSwiney

KDP – AMAZON Press

TTT

https://www.timetotransform.com.au

Title: Chifley and Australian Post War Reconstruction: The Australian Labor Party and the Federal Platform 1945-1949 / Dr John McSwiney, author.

ISBN: 9798639896125

Cover and internal design by Dr John McSwiney

Typeset in Baskerville 12/24

This fifth book in the series is dedicated to the Australian Labor Party and all who support it.

CONTENTS

ACKNOWLEDGMENTS

I am not sure where I got my love of politics but I can still remember the day my father was yelling at the television when Gough Whitlam was sacked: that was interesting!

Thankyou to my parents for instilling in me the value of labour and the importance of standing up for your rights.

Thankyou to my family for loving my eccentricities and putting up with me, including my antics on election day and the ritual watching of the human psephologist Antony Green on the ABC and the theatre of him drilling into the minutia, booth by booth and seat by seat! Love it!

Thankyou to my political heroes growing up, the Hon. Bob Hawke; the Hon. Paul Keating and the Hon. John Cain. All men of vision who understood the importance of the big picture as well as representing working men and women across Australia.

Thankyou to my university professors who entertained me over many years with a myriad of stories and anecdotes and who were passionate about politics, its role in society and the greater good that could be achieved through it. The three most notable and influential were Dennis Woodward; Brian Costar and Derek Verrall. I am indebted to all of you.

Thankyou to all my friends in politics and the trade union movement who I journeyed with for many years. Always fighting the good fight and never giving up. It was great to be a part of and has provided me with countless memories and many smiles.

1 INTRODUCTION

Book number five in the series of Labor and the Platform analyses the emergence of Ben Chifley from Labor Treasurer to Labor leader following the death of John Curtin and the issues and challenges that faced the government in rebuilding Australia after spending five years fighting a world war. Labor controlled both Houses during Chifley's time in office and the control of the Senate was pivotal in Labor's success of enacting the platform. Labor's success during the period is comparable with the achievements of Fisher's second administration between 1910-1913. Chifley governed in a world rebuilding itself after a global conflict and with the nation's focus on the home front Chifley legislated accordingly. However, unfortunately for Chifley and Labor and like Labor governments like Fisher before him, the major obstacle to Labor enacting the entire platform was a combination of High Court interpretations of legislation and the constraints of the Constitution in respect of referendum proposals.

On 26 April 1945 John Curtin chaired his last Caucus meeting. On 29 April he was admitted to hospital with 'congestion on the lungs'[1] and as Deputy Prime Minister Forde was in the USA Chifley became acting Prime Minister. On 10 May Chifley reported to Caucus on Curtin's health:

> Mr Curtin was doing very well and was much improved and should at an early date be able to leave hospital ... he had advised the Prime Minister that it was the Party's opinion and wish that he should take a complete holiday before returning to his place in Parliament.[2]

Curtin's health had been deteriorating for a while and although he chaired Caucus and attended the start of the parliamentary session in February 1945, he was not the same man that led Labor into government in 1941. Curtin's decline forced Chifley into the spotlight and he took control of steering Labor's policy agenda through the Parliament, with Crisp noting:

> As the seriousness of Curtin's condition became known, parliamentarians and correspondents watched Chifley's leadership with a new fascination. There could have been no more testing conditions. With Curtin, Forde and Evatt absent, Chifley had to call on the barely convalescent Beasley to shoulder for the time being the portfolios of Defence and Attorney-General as well as Supply; he himself was Acting Prime Minister, Treasurer and (briefly) Acting External Affairs Minister.[3]

---

[1] Day, _op cit._, p.567.
[2] _Caucus Minutes_, 10 May 1945.
[3] Crisp, 1961, _op cit._, p.219.

2 WWII ENDS AND RECONSTRUCTION COMMENCES

Labor commenced the 1945 parliamentary session with a flurry of activity enacting fifty-nine separate legislative Acts, including the following key policy planks of the platform:

- nationalising Australia's airlines (plank 4(b) – Methods Section);

- extending government controls over private trading banks (plank 4(a) – Methods Section);

- establishing a system of subsidised housing (plank 17 – Social Reform Section);

- implementing a system of uniform divorce laws (plank 15 – Social Reform Section);

- expanding and building the Northern Territory (plank 13 – Economic Section);

- establishing a comprehensive Life Insurance program (plank 16 – Social Reform Section); and

- introducing a comprehensive Pharmaceutical Benefits scheme for all Australians (plank 4(d) – Methods Section);

The 1945 session provided the foundation on which the Government's overall pursuit of the platform would be based and a little over two weeks after the session commenced the Government introduced two complementary Bills that sought to redefine the banking system in Australia in line with plank 4(a) of the platform.

<u>Commonwealth Bank</u>

The introduction of the controversial Banking legislation left little doubt that Labor meant business, however in respect of banking, these two Bills were only a portent of what was to come. Labor's banking planks were firmly entrenched in the platform and although the Government had introduced regulations that tightened the Government's control over the banks, they did not seek to replace the regulations with legislation during the war. However, at the 16th Commonwealth Conference in 1943 the report of the Finance Committee highlighted that:

> Since the Labor Government had been in office much had been done by regulation to bring banking under the Commonwealth Bank.[4]

Taylor elucidated on the ambit of the regulations, informing delegates that:

> No other country in the world exercised the same control

---

[4] Australian Labor Party, <u>Official Report of Proceedings of the 16th Commonwealth Conference</u>, Sydney, 16 December 1943, p.31.

over banking. The Commonwealth Parliament had sufficient powers in the Constitution to control banking in line with the party's policy. The only other desirable power lacking was in regard to control of overseas exchange. [5]

Chifley was aware of the sensitive nature of the proposals and he drafted 'explanatory notes' in connection with each Bill.[6] Chifley did not want to leave anything to chance, however Caucus wasted little time in expressing their preferred policy options in respect of nationalising the banks in line with Plank 4(a) of the Platform with Burke unsuccessfully moving that:

> The present Bills be withdrawn and a Bill introduced giving the Government power to acquire the business and assets of the private trading banks as a going concern. [7]

After Burke's motion failed, he seconded a motion from Ward that proposed:

> That the licensing provision be amended to provide that
> the Government, being the authority which issues the
> licence permitting the operations of a private bank, be also
> the authority which may withdraw the licence for
> continued and flagrant failure to carry out the obligations
> contained in the Regulations. [8]

Burke and Ward's motions were defeated but they were a trumpet call to action. The Banking Bills formed the basis for Labor to pursue the banking platform *en masse*. For the first time since

---

[5] ibid.

[6] Chifley then told his colleagues to write their names on the copies he had given them and to treat them as confidential. He also requested that they hand them in at the adjournment and when the debate on the Bills had concluded they were to hand them to the Whip. See, *Caucus Minutes*, 19 February 1945.

[7] *Caucus Minutes*, 20 February 1945.

[8] ibid.

Fisher in 1914 Labor was in a realistic position to pursue the banking platform and Chifley did not waste his opportunity to make significant reforms in line with key policy planks of the platform. Les Haylen, one of Chifley's colleagues outlined Chifley's rationale for introducing the Commonwealth Bank Bill 1945:

> Deep in Chifley's heart was a burning resentment of the things done to Prime Minister Scullin in London when during the depression he went cap in hand to the Bank of England and Montague Norman for a paltry 20 million pounds to see us through. This was flatly rejected and was followed by the Premier's Plan, the most contemptible piece of planned misery and dole psychology ever to be passed by Australian parliaments.[9]

The Commonwealth Bank Bill 1945 proposed to strengthen the central banking functions of the Commonwealth Bank, thus ensuring that the Commonwealth Bank's policies would be in sync with the Government's. Chifley had been a proponent for change in the Banking Industry as he had seen and experienced the egregious way in which the Australian banks had conducted business during the depression period and this was reflected in his minority report on Banking to the Royal Commission on Banking in 1936. Also, the social reforms Chifley wished to pursue, the main one being 'full employment', could not be implemented unless the Commonwealth Bank Bill 1945 became law. On 9 March 1945 Chifley introduced the Bills into the House:

> At the present time, when we are facing a future that is full of problems involving momentous economic issues, any legislation affecting the banking system always must be in

---

[9] Haylen, L., Twenty Years Hard Labor. McMillan & Co. Pty. Ltd. Melbourne, Australia, 1969, p.43.

process of evolution, continuously adapting itself to changing conditions … The legislation that I am proposing today is based on the conviction that the Government must accept responsibility for the economic condition of the nation. The problems of the post-war period – of employment, development and trade, are of such magnitude, and involve such serious consequences, that no other attitude could be maintained. Accordingly, the Government has decided to assume the powers which are necessary over banking policy to assist it in maintaining national economic health and prosperity.[10]

At the end of the second reading on the Commonwealth Bank Bill he sought leave [which was granted] to proceed with the Banking Bill:

> The purpose of this Bill is to regulate banking and to make provision for the protection of the currency and the public credit of the Commonwealth. The regulation of the banking system is an essential accompaniment to the revision of Commonwealth Bank powers … In fact, the reform of the trading bank system was one of the main themes of the report of the Royal Commission on Monetary and Banking Systems, and the principal subject of its various recommendations … The war intervened before any of these recommendations were acted upon, and some re-consideration of the report of the commission has become necessary in consequence of the changes that have occurred in the banking system during the war.[11]

The Commonwealth Bank Bill sought to repeal all previous Acts in order to establish new functions and powers for the Bank. The Bill

---

[10] *C.P.D.*, Vol. 181, 9 March 1945, p.546-7.
[11] ibid., p.553.

established a new departmental framework to streamline Banking operations, with each Department being responsible for a specific core banking function such as: Mortgage Bank, Industrial Finance, Commonwealth Savings Bank, Rural Credit and the Note Issue. The Bill also prescribed the Bank's status as a 'Central Bank' that would be authorised and required to carry out general banking business in competition with other banks in line with its new Departmental structure. The Bill sought to abolish the Commonwealth Bank Board with management of the institution being placed in the hands of a Governor, who would receive policy directives from the Treasurer and the Government.

The Commonwealth Bank Bill overhauled the operational parameters in which the Bank carried out its business. The Bank would be established as the Central Bank in the system, and the Government's Banking Bill placed the control of the system under the Commonwealth Bank. The Bill provided the Commonwealth Bank with the power to control interest rates in the banking system as well as restructuring how and with whom non-government trading banks would do business.[12] The Bill also required the non-government trading banks to place a percentage of their reserve capital, called 'special deposits' with the Commonwealth Bank. The Government's banking legislation was extensive and even though the legislation stopped short of nationalising the system in line with plank 4(a) of the platform, the proposals sought to enact almost the entire banking platform contained in the section entitled 'Progressive Reforms', as well as the planks outlined in the 'Plan of Action' section of the Platform:

PROGRESSIVE REFORMS

---

[12] The Banking Bill prohibited non-government trading banks from conducting banking business for States and State Authorities, however this provision was challenged in the High Court and found to be unconstitutional. See; *City of Melbourne v Commonwealth (State Banking Case)* 74 C.L.R. 31.

1.   The Commonwealth Bank to be developed on the following lines:

(a)   A nation wide Trading Bank handling the ordinary business of the community. *(Commonwealth Bank Act 1945)*

(b)   A Savings-Bank performing the ordinary functions of such a Bank; *(Commonwealth Bank Act 1945)* and

Plan Of Action

(1)   The operations of the Commonwealth Bank to be removed from and made entirely independent of private banking interests and free from sectional influences or constraint. *(Commonwealth Bank Act 1945)*

(2)   The abolition of the Commonwealth Bank Board and the re-establishment of the original method of control as set up- at the time the Commonwealth Bank was founded. *(Commonwealth Bank Act 1945)*

(3)   Expansion of the bank's business as a trading bank, with branches in all suitable centres, in vigorous competition with the private banking establishments. *(Commonwealth Bank Act 1945)*

(4)   A statutory provision that the banking of all public bodies shall be reserved for the Commonwealth Bank.[13] *(Banking Act 1945)*

The Bills came under immediate attack by members of the Liberal Party and the banking industry. Of particular note were the

---

[13] Australian Labor Party, <u>Official Report of Proceedings of the 16th Commonwealth Conference</u>, Sydney, 16 December 1943, p.4-5.

Associated Banks who not only launched a scathing attack on the legislation, but also a veiled personal attack on Chifley stating:

> The Banking Bills introduced into the House of Representatives by the Treasurer have, unfortunately, justified the misgivings which have been apparent in the community since it became known that such legislation was proposed. One stands aghast at the revolutionary provisions of the Bills and the possible effect they could have on the economic health of the country and the well-being of its citizens.
>
> All other provisions of the Bills pale into insignificance when it is realised that control of the nation's credit and currency would vest in one man – the Treasurer of the day … The possibilities that this opens up are so alarming that it is difficult to understand that any democratic Government should desire to open the way to them. It is to be deplored that such highly contentious and potentially dangerous proposals should be brought forward to disturb the public mind in these days of war.[14]

The Opposition followed the lead of the Associated Banks, with Menzies focusing on the issue of the establishment of a 'central bank' and its functions in the proposed system stating:

> The whole proposal on this point is a striking example of the Government's desire to perpetuate in Australia, long after the emergencies have passed, what has been epigrammatically styled "the servile state", and the particular weapon here is the weapon of slow strangulation of the private banking system in favour of a publicly owned and politically controlled banking system.[15]

---

[14] *The Age*, 12 March 1945.

Menzies' comments were measured in comparison to the Leader of the Country Party, Fadden, who was openly scathing of the socialistic nature of the Bill:

> This measure, revolutionary though it may be, is only consistent with the policy of the Labor Party, and the basic desire of that party to convert Australia into a socialistic state … Actually for many years' past, the Labor Party has endeavored to pass sentence of death on the private trading banking institutions of Australia, and to gain political control of the banking system.[16]

Calwell was quick to remind Fadden during his speech that:

> … this Bill does not propose nationalisation of banking … [to which Fadden replied] … No, it does worse than that; it proposes strangulation of private banking.[17]

The Opposition and the banking and financial sectors provided trenchant resistance to the Banking Bills. However, despite the opposition the Government refused to back down and it passed the Bills into law strengthening key banking planks in the platform. Two months after the banking Bills were debated in the Parliament, Chifley had the honour, as acting Prime Minister, to inform the country that Germany had surrendered to the Allies. Chifley had received news of the surrender a day before in a top secret cablegram from London on 7 May 1945 that stated:

> The surrender of all German Forces in Europe to Allied Expeditionary Force and the Soviet High Command was signed at 0141 hours this morning, Monday 7th May by representatives of the   German High Command and

---

[15] *C.P.D.*, Vol. 181, 21 March 1945, p.752.
[16] ibid., p.783.
[17] *C.P.D.*, Vol. 181, 22 March 1945, p.785.

General Eisenhower and General Suslaparov to take effect midnight Tuesday-Wednesday May 8-9th. Please treat above with complete secrecy for the moment. No release of the news is being made pending simultaneous announcement by the United Kingdom, United States and Soviet Governments. This is at present fixed for 3 p.m. B.S.T. Tuesday 8th May. If any change in this arrangement is made I will let you know at once.[18]

The German surrender, or V.E day, on 8 May 1945 had come at a heavy cost to the nation and although Australia rejoiced, celebrations were tempered somewhat by the fact that Australia was still at war with Japan. The war in the Pacific was still being waged, however this did not stop the Government proceeding with its legislative agenda to pursue and enact the platform.

Life Insurance

In late May Chifley introduced the Life Insurance Bill, another important piece of legislation which covered a key part of plank 16 in the Social Reform section of the Platform:

> National Insurance, including provision for sick, accident, life and unemployment insurance, to include benefits to the dependents of the persons insured.[19]

A National Insurance scheme was the stated goal of the platform, with plank 16 being amended at the 15th Commonwealth Conference in May 1939 to include 'benefits to the dependents of the persons insured'.[20] The Bill was the first piece of insurance

---

[18] Cablegram D769 LONDON, 7 May 1945, 10.19 a.m. [AA:A1066, H45/1013/2/2/2] located at: http://www.info.dfat.gov.au/info/historical/HistDocs.nsf/vVolume/AA8726E O249A0F8I

[19] Australian Labor Party, Official Report of Proceedings of the 16th Commonwealth Conference, Sydney, 16 December 1943, p.4.

legislation introduced by Labor since it came to power and although being limited in its scope in relation to the platform it was still a positive step towards stated policy goals. On 25 May Chifley explained to the House that the purpose of the Bill was to:

> ... regulate life insurance business conducted in Australia, and to protect the interests of persons who have effected life insurance policies ... It has long been recognised that some form of public control is necessary over a business which affects such a large proportion of the people.[21]

Chifley then provided a brief history of life insurance legislation in Australia and posited that it was the intent of the Bill to 'consolidate the existing State and Commonwealth Acts',[22] and that the Bill had four main objectives:

(a)   To replace all State legislation on the subject of life insurance, and to provide a uniform basis for applying the requirements of those acts to the whole of Australia.

(b)   To incorporate existing Commonwealth acts with minor amendments.

(c)   To appoint an insurance commissioner who shall exercise active supervision of the activities of life insurance companies, with a view to securing the greatest possible protection for policy owners.

---

[20] Australian Labor Party, <u>Official Report of Proceedings of the 15th Commonwealth Conference</u>, Canberra, 5 May 1939, p.71-2.
[21] *C.P.D.*, Vol. 182, 25 May 1945, p.2144.
[22] <u>ibid.</u>, p.2145.

(d)   To set up adequate machinery for dealing with any company that fails to maintain a required minimum standard of solvency.[23]

The debate and subsequent passage of the Bill was the last piece of legislation, based on the platform, that Curtin would have noted prior to his death on 5 July 1945. Curtin's death had not been unexpected, however when it happened it sent shockwaves through the Government and the wider labour movement. Chifley had led Labor since the start of the session and was instrumental in guiding the legislative program through the Parliament, however even though Labor did not have an official succession plan, it was Forde (Deputy Prime Minister) who was 'next in line' for the leadership, not Chifley.

Forde had been in America as one of Australia's representatives at the opening of the United Nations and had only arrived back in Australia three days prior to Curtin's death. Forde was duly sworn in by the Governor General as caretaker Prime Minister until Caucus elected a new leader. On Thursday 12 July Caucus assembled to vote for one of three candidates who had nominated for the leadership: Forde, Chifley and Makin.

When Caucus assembled to vote on the leadership a number of members were absent, the most notable being Evatt who was on board a ship in the middle of the Pacific returning to Australia.[24] Caucus members had noted the absentees and Williams moved:

That the election of Leader be postponed until the return of Dr. Evatt, Mr Pollard and Senator Nash.[25]

---

[23] *C.P.D.*, Vol. 182, 25 May 1945, p.2145-6.

[24] Evatt had taken a holiday after attending the United Nations opening with Forde, unfortunately for Evatt, he was in a ship in the Pacific and the war with Japan was still being waged, the ship was bound by radio silence and a message of proceedings in Australia had to be dropped to him.

Williams' motion failed for want of a seconder, however James moved:

> That owing to the absence of so many members of the party from the meeting:

> 1. That the present Prime Minister, Mr Forde, and the Cabinet carry on for a period of five weeks as from today.

> 2. At this meeting we then proceed only to elect a Leader and fill the vacant Cabinet position.

> 3. In the meantime, we request Cabinet to give consideration to recommending to Caucus the appointment of Assistants to those Ministers who are overworked, on similar lines to those adopted by the New Zealand Labor Government.

> 4. This question to be decided by secret ballot.[26]

James' motion was defeated and then Marten's moved as an amendment:

> 1. That the eighteen members of the Cabinet be re-appointed.

> 2. That we proceed to elect the Leader and then to elect a Minister to fill the Cabinet vacancy caused by the death of Mr Curtin.

> 3. That this matter be decided by ballot.[27]

---

[25] *Caucus Minutes*, 12 July 1945.
[26] ibid.
[27] ibid.

James' motion was ruled out of order by the Chair. In the ensuing vote Chifley received forty-four votes, Forde sixteen, Makin eight and Evatt one. According to the Caucus minutes Chifley then thanked his colleagues 'for the honour they had confirmed on him'[28] and stated that he:

> ... would give of his best at all times and asked members for their co-operation in all matters, as success could only be assured if this were done.[29]

Chifley's victory was decisive, however according to Crisp, Chifley's time as acting Prime Minister whilst Forde was in America played a pivotal role in his victory:

> For Chifley's career the two months of May and June 1945, proved crucial. Forde's performances during his two periods as Acting Prime Minister in the previous twelve months had been conscientious but unimpressive. An able, likeable politician, he had neither the intellectual power and range nor the ready command of the many branches of Government business compared with Curtin and Chifley.[30]

Forde's defeat was a bitter personal blow, as he had been the Deputy Labor leader since 1935. Haylen, in his book 'Twenty Years Hard Labor' recalled the conversation he had had with Forde on the morning before the vote:

> He asked me about his chances. I told him frankly what the position was. It was brutal but it was the kindest thing to do. I saw a different Frank Forde. His face went deathly white, the veins on his neck stood out in an effort to suppress his emotions. No man gives up the Prime

---

[28] ibid.
[29] ibid.
[30] Crisp, 1961, op cit, p.219.

Ministership easily. After a while he said, "I must say a little prayer for Ben. It's not an easy job".[31]

Chifley assumed the leadership and Forde was elected as deputy leader by an almost unanimous margin.[32] Four days after being elected by Caucus, Chifley addressed Labor's Macquarie District Assembly in New South Wales calling for the party to unite:

> The Party will not stand for dissension in any movement, Labor or otherwise, that seeks to govern this country ... [he] did not desire the Labor movement to become a mutual admiration society ... to him Labor was a social religion for the betterment of mankind.[33]

The Development of Northern Australia

In the hours prior to Curtin's death the Government introduced important legislation based on plank 13 of the Platform for the 'Development and settlement of Northern Australia'.[34] The bombing of Darwin on 22 April 1942 had brought the war to Australia's shores causing the evacuation of much of its civilian population and the area ostensibly became a military base of operations. In July 1945 with the war heading to an end the Government took proactive steps to prepare for the resettling of Darwin for the civilian population and took another step to enact an important plank of the platform. On 4 July 1945 Lazzarini outlined the Government's plans for Darwin in the Darwin Lands Acquisition Bill:

---

[31] Haylen, op cit, p.67.

[32] Evatt and Forde contested the Deputy Leader's position. The final vote was Forde 68 votes and Evatt 1 or 2.

[33] *Bathurst National Advocate*, 16 July 1945.

[34] Australian Labor Party, Official Report of Proceedings of the 16th Commonwealth Conference, Sydney, 16 December 1943, p.7.

> This short measure is designed to authorise the acquisition by the Commonwealth of freehold land in the town of Darwin and its environs … As a result of the bombing of Darwin, many of the houses and buildings were destroyed. Other property has been demolished to meet defence requirements. The whole of Darwin's "Chinatown" has disappeared. The carefully considered view of a number of authorities is that all freehold land in the Darwin area should be acquired by the Commonwealth …The acquisition is desirable to enable the future development of Darwin and the exploitation of its potentialities to the best advantage, from both civilian and defence points of view.[35]

The Bill was an important measure pursued by Labor to ensure that after the war, there would be a viable system in place to redevelop industry and settle civilians in Darwin and its environs in line with stated platform policy goals. The Bill was later followed by the *Northern Territory (Administration) Act* in 1947 and the *Northern Territory Representation Act* in 1949. All three pieces of legislation aimed to create a strong and viable environment for civilian settlement and business development that changed the face of Northern Australia and provided the Government with another plank of the platform legislated into law.

Nationalisation of Australian Airlines

On the same day that Lazzarini introduced legislation to rebuild Darwin, Drakeford requested that leave be granted:

> … to bring in a Bill for an act to provide for the establishment and operation of a national airline service by the Commonwealth.[36]

---

[35] *C.P.D.*, Vol. 183, 4 July 1945, p.4049.
[36] ibid.

Labor had already successfully introduced Banking legislation earlier in the session, now it was proposing to nationalise Australia's airlines. The Australian National Airlines Bill 1945 was introduced in line with plank 4(b) of the platform that called for the 'Nationalising of Monopolies'.[37] The Australian National Airlines Bill 1945 was one of the few legislative initiatives since federation that actually advocated the nationalisation of an industry in line with stated policy planks of the platform. Labor had only spent about thirteen years in government since 1901 and with the exception of a number of abortive attempts to reform the banking industry, this Bill was the first active pursuit of the platform 'Objective' in a coherent form. On 18 July 1945, Drakeford, the Minister for Air and Civil Aviation, addressed the issue of monopolies in the airline industry when he introduced the Bill stating:

> The proper approach to this legislation should be: Is it in the interests of the people as a whole? Is national ownership and control of civil aviation preferable to a private monopoly? These are the real questions, for there is abundant evidence that a monopoly is inevitable in the near future.[38]

> Labor was committed to eliminating the virtual monopoly that existed in the airline industry and set out four main objectives to achieve this goal:

> The social obligation, the economic obligation, national development and national defence.[39]

The Government was also well aware of the fact that the legislation

---

[37] Australian Labor Party, <u>Official Report of Proceedings of the 16th Commonwealth Conference</u>, Sydney, 16 December 1943, p.4.
[38] *C.P.D.*, Vol. 183, 18 July 1945, p.4179.
[39] <u>ibid.</u>, p.4181.

would reignite hostilities over Labor's 'Socialist' policy agenda that came to the fore on the debate on the bank legislation, when Drakeford stated:

> I anticipate that the Honourable members opposite will attack it from the same political party angle as they used in attacking the banking Bills … No doubt the word socialisation will echo through every speech in this debate from honourable members opposite – socialisation, with all the dread foreboding they can conjure. But I would remind them that had this nation depended on private enterprise to organise the country for war, we would not have accomplished one fraction of the marvelous war effort achieved in this grave crisis … I recognise that there exists in certain sections of the community and in the minds of some honourable members opposite, a predetermined hostility. Because of this I make the strongest possible plea for reasoned thinking. If that is granted I have no doubt that the debate which will follow will be profitable, and that the House will pass the Bill as a constructive piece of legislation.[40]

Drakeford's plea for reasoned thinking was ignored by Menzies who summed up his and his party's position on the Bill:

> … the Government, without analysis, without reasoning without any true technical support, has introduced a Bill simply to give effect to its party constitution. Nationalisation is the Government's policy; therefore, let the airlines be nationalised. Has there been any examination of the facts? No. Has technical advice been received supporting the conclusion reached by the Government? No. Nationalisation is in the party constitution; therefore, it is to be proceeded with.

---

[40] ibid., p.4178-9.

> Therefore, the choice is either a dull adherence to academic socialist theory for its own sake or a realistic approach to the actual and rapidly changing needs of the people in the world of modern transport and communications.[41]

Menzies' view was also backed up by Spender, who attacked the Bill's socialist bent as well as taking the opportunity to introduce Communist Russia into the debate:

> ... I turn now to the so-called merits of the Bill ... An examination discloses that there is only one real purpose. The idea of the Government that socialisation of anything must be for the benefit of the people is outmoded. It has become almost fashionable to speak about the great prowess of Russia, as though its economic system were better than that of any other country ... Socialisation or nationalisation, or government ownership, is not the best means of raising the standard of living of the people ... The Bill cannot be shown to have one merit.[42]

Burke[43] and Fuller spoke in support of the Bill with Fuller staking his political reputation on the legislation:

> This is one of the most important Bills ever presented to the House and I wholeheartedly support it. In fact, I am prepared to stake my political neck upon it.[44]

Fuller kept his neck and the Bill was passed through the Parliament, establishing an Airlines Commission with the express power to control interstate civil aviation as well as setting up the

---

[41] *C.P.D.*, Vol. 184, 25 July 1945, pp.4556-7.
[42] *C.P.D.*, Vol. 184, 27 July 1945, pp.4690-3.
[43] See; ibid., pp.4697-02
[44] ibid., p.4708.

government's own flagship carrier, Trans-Australian Airlines (TAA), to conduct interstate air services. The legislation also provided for the termination of all privately owned airline carriers operating interstate air services in competition with TAA. However, a challenge by non-government airline operators was upheld by the High Court that found the legislation to be unconstitutional and thus impacting on Labor's plan to break the airline monopoly and nationalise the industry.[45] The discretionary clauses contained in the Act provided the Government with the power to cancel (or not renew) private airline licences, thus eliminating other carriers in competition with the Government sponsored carrier, TAA. The High Court's ruling on the discretionary power contained in the Act was a setback to the Government's plans to legislate for its stated platform policy on nationalisation, however despite the High Court's judgement, the Government continued to pursue the platform.

Marriage and Divorce

The nation's focus was on the nationalisation of Australia's airlines when the Government introduced more legislation relating to the platform. Major reforms in banking and the airlines were not the Government's only policy initiatives to bring the platform into law, it now introduced legislation for marriage and divorce. Plank 15 of the platform related to the issue of 'Uniform Laws of Marriage and Divorce',[46] and the Matrimonial Causes Bill introduced by Chifley was the first piece of legislation on marriage or divorce, in the federal jurisdiction, since the passage of the *Matrimonial Causes (Dominion Troops) Act* 1919.[47] According to Chifley the objects of

---

[45] See; *Australian National Airways Pty Ltd and ors. V Commonwealth* (October-November 1945) 71 C.L.R. 29

[46] Australian Labor Party, <u>Official Report of Proceedings of the 16th Commonwealth Conference</u>, Sydney, 16 December 1943, p.7.

[47] *C.P.D.*, Vol. XC, 17 October 1919, pp.13548-9.

the Bill were twofold:

> First, to enable an Australian woman married to an overseas serviceman or other person from overseas to institute divorce proceedings in Australia; and, secondly, to provide that a person domiciled anywhere in Australia may institute divorce proceedings in the State or Territory in which he or she is for the time being resident.[48]

The Bill only focused on the 'divorce' aspect of the plank and did not pursue the subject of 'uniform laws of marriage'. The subject was raised by the Liberal, Holt during debate when he interjected during Chifley's speech:

> I suggest that consideration should be given to a general Australian marriage law, not merely a divorce law.[49]

Chifley replied that, 'The honourable member must realise that it is a "sticky" subject'. Chifley then discussed the outcomes of an earlier Premiers' Conference meeting on the subject and informed the House that:

> I propose to leave my learned colleague, the Attorney General (Mr Evatt), upon his return, to argue the difficult points raised by ... the honourable member for Fawkner (Mr. Holt). I realise my limitations. [50]

Evatt addressed the legal aspects of the Bill and provided responses to Opposition questions. In relation to the question of marriage Evatt stated:

> Marriage, has, first a religious significance of a sacramental

---

[48] *C.P.D.*, Vol. 184, 20 July 1945, p.4350.
[49] ibid., p.4352.
[50] ibid., pp.4352-3.

or almost sacramental character, according to the views of the churches, and, secondly, a tremendously important social significance. My own opinion is that nothing could be worse for a country than to weaken the institution of marriage by making divorce too easy.[51]

Evatt's legal expertise was acknowledged by the Opposition and the Bill passed through the remaining stages without amendment, thus ensuring another important plank in the platform was enacted during the session. Chifley had been at the forefront of the Government's legislative agenda and was responsible for driving through major reforms related to the platform. In the middle of the session Chifley also had the fitting opportunity to inform the people of Australia that Japan had surrendered. On 15 August 1945, in a radio broadcast to the nation, Chifley announced Japan's surrender:

> Fellow citizens, the war is over.
>
> The Japanese government has accepted the terms of surrender imposed by the Allied Nations and hostilities will now cease. The reply by the Japanese government to the note sent by Britain, the United States, the U.S.S.R and China has been received and accepted by the Allied nations.[52]

Chifley then discussed the return of the troops from the theatres of war as well as the new United Nations Charter, he then turned his thoughts towards the rebuilding of Australia:

> Here in Australia, there is much to be done. The Australian government, which stood steadfast during the

---

[51] *C.P.D.*, Vol. 184, 1 August 1945, p.4841.
[52] Chifley, B., <u>Things Worth Fighting For: Speeches by Joseph Benedict Chifley</u>. Melbourne University Press, 1952, p12.

dread days of war, will give all that it has to working and planning to ensure that the peace will be a real thing. I ask that the State governments and all sections of the community should cooperate in facing the tasks and solving the problems that are ahead. Let us join together in the march of our nation to future greatness.[53]

The general feeling of the Australian community to the announcement was no where better captured than in an *Age* article the following day:

> Wistful, joyous, sad, exuberant, perplexed, sorrowful, delirious, wild, these citizens sighed, sang and shouted their relief that war – the second world war within thirty years – had ended. It was a celebration of strange, confusing, violent, emotional import that will long be remembered. Nothing like it in sheer eruption that may – we hope and pray – never again be witnessed. It was tempest after storm.[54]

There was little doubt that the world in which Labor now found itself would be different from what it had experienced in the preceding four years. Labor had governed in war, now it had to govern for the peace.

Public Health – Hospital Benefits and Tuberculosis

The constraints that Labor was under in fighting the war were no longer present and the opportunity to pursue the platform, without having to fight a war, was a strong driver to enact stated party policy and in September 1945 the Government moved to legislate in the area of Public Health and strengthen its commitment to key

---

[53] ibid., p14.
[54] *The Age*, 16 August 1945.

planks of the platform with the introduction of the Hospital Benefits Bill and the Tuberculosis Bill. The Tuberculosis Bill provided grants to the States to conduct a campaign to identify and treat the disease. The Hospital Benefits Bill was introduced by Lazzarini and was regarded by him as:

> ... a further major step in developing the Government's health and social services policy.[55]

The Hospital Bill provided for tied grants to the States to subsidise the costs of maintaining their public hospitals. The Grants were conditional on the hospitals providing accommodation, treatment and services free of charge for specified areas. The legislation provided important health benefits to Australians, however although the Government had not pursued a policy of outright nationalisation of the health system as stated in plank 4(d) of the platform, its initiatives in respect of Pharmaceutical Benefits, Hospital Benefits and its Tuberculosis measures had provided Australians with a level of health care far superior than before these initiatives were introduced and strengthened Labor's position on nationalising the system in line with the platform.

Commonwealth Housing Scheme

The 1945 session was significant for Labor, as the Government had delivered a number of key planks in the platform, the most notable being the Banking reforms and nationalising Australia's Airlines. Another key plank was added to Labor's list of achievements with the establishment of a national housing scheme. In April 1943 the Curtin Government appointed a Commonwealth Housing Commission within the Ministry of Post-war Reconstruction. The Commission visited all states and obtained exhaustive information and evidence from every section of the community. The

---

[55] *C.P.D.*, Vol. 184, 12 September 1945, p.5299.

Commission published three reports with the final report being tabled in Parliament in September 1945. The Commission considered that governments should take an active part in providing housing and that the Commonwealth Government should supplement the housing activities of State governments:

> (The Commission) argued, in its final report, for a broad-based and comprehensive approach to housing policy, … with a national target of 80,000 dwellings per year. Such an ambitious target would require cooperation between government and private sectors and co-ordination between the various levels of government. The federal government was to assume the primary financial burden, in keeping with its greatly augmented revenue-raising capacity … The Commonwealth would also monitor and consider housing provision within a comprehensive national economic planning framework, … Public works programs would be coordinated through regular Premiers' Conferences and Loan Council meetings. In this scenario the state governments would be directly responsible tor the construction and management of the expanding public housing sector.[56]

On 16 December 1943, eight months after Labor appointed the Commonwealth Housing Commission, delegates at the 16th Commonwealth Conference urged the Government to initiate a housing scheme for rural districts as a complementary factor to decentralisation, successfully moving that:

> The Government appoint a Commonwealth General Construction Authority for the purposes of:

---

[56] Hayward, D., The Reluctant Landlords? A history of Public Housing in Australia, 1996, p.6. see: http://www.infoxchange.net.au/rhchome/iurhc/index.htm

a) Clearance of slum areas, and siting of suitable areas and locations for groups of homes, townships and new suburbs, and provision of community facilities.

b) Developing modern types and standards of dwellings, and consolidation of minimum standards in a National Housing Code.

c) Promoting home ownership.

d) Providing housing for rental.[57]

Delegates also re-approved plank 17 of the 'Social Reform' section of the platform that outlined the party's position with respect to providing quality housing to working families by simply stating that Labor would pursue, 'An adequate housing scheme'.[58] The plank was simple, however the Government's total commitment to the war effort precluded it from appropriating the necessary capital to fund such a scheme. However, the tabling of the final report of the Commission in September 1945 coupled with the fact that the war was over provided Labor with an opportunity to implement this key social reform plank. On 13 September 1945, Dedman, Minister for Post War Reconstruction, introduced the Commonwealth and State Housing Agreement Bill into Parliament to enact plank 17 of the Social Reform section of the platform:

> The Bill … is an important piece of social legislation. It will provide means whereby a full scale attack can be made on one of the worst of our social evils, namely, the bad housing of the Australian people.
>
> … this Bill provides a plan for housing and rehousing

---

[57] Australian Labor Party, <u>Official Report of Proceedings of the 16th Commonwealth Conference</u>, Sydney, 16 December 1943, p.38.
[58] <u>ibid.</u>, p.7.

> families of the lower income group, adequately, effectively and hygienically on a scale in advance of all our past performances … the principal deficiency in Australian housing policy to date has been in respect of good standard houses to be let at rents within their capacity to pay, to families who cannot afford, or are not ready, or on account of their occupations do not desire, to purchase homes. To our great discredit, there has not been to date a full scale attack on our slums …

> The Government realises the need for the encouragement of home ownership. The Commonwealth Bank Act, which was recently enacted, and the War Service Homes Act are ample proof of the Commonwealth's interest in that matter.[59]

The Bill strengthened the Government's commitment to enacting the social reform planks in its platform and now that the war had ended the Government was in a strong position to pursue important policy planks such as providing adequate housing to those who needed it most. The *Commonwealth and State Housing Agreement Act* 1945 established a housing scheme involving both State and Federal governments subsidising the construction of homes for particular sections of the Australian community. On 3 October 1945 the Government introduced the Loan (Housing) Bill and Lazarrini informed the House that:

> The purpose of this Bill is to obtain a loan appropriation of £15,000,000 to be applied in making advances to the States of Capital funds for housing under the Commonwealth and State housing agreements. Under the agreements, the Commonwealth will advance the initial capital funds to the States, subject to stated conditions as to interest and repayments.[60]

---

[59] *C.P.D.*, Vol. 184, 13 September 1945, pp.5385-6.

The appropriation Bill provided the financial stimulus required for the commencement of the program with £10,500,000 being allocated for the 1945-6 year. The balance of the funds being allocated to the States following ratification of the agreement. The funds were now available to pursue policy initiatives like housing because the Government was no longer committed to stringent economic management based on full war production.

The 1945 parliamentary session would go down in Labor annals as one of the most bitter sweet in Labor's history. The year had seen the death of John Curtin, the rise of Ben Chifley and the end of the second world war, however despite the momentous changes, the Government maintained its focus on the legislative tasks at hand. With the war over and the task of post war reconstruction commencing, Labor's advance of the platform would take on an added significance.

The 1946 parliamentary session commenced in March and Labor wasted little time in governing for the peace. Chifley was Prime Minister in his own right, but was still to face the people at an election. The war had ended with an Allied victory and Labor had carriage of rebuilding the nation. In the period from March to September 1946 Labor enacted fifty-five pieces of legislation with Labor's legislative program containing a number of amending Acts that strengthened and updated key social reform and health planks of the platform. Planks 17, 18 and 19 of the Social Reform agenda relating to 'adequate housing', 'widows' pensions' and 'invalid and old age pensions' were boosted by the passage of the *Invalid and Old Age Pensions Act* 1946 the *Widows' Pensions Act* 1946 and the *Loan (Housing) Act* 1946. Also, plank 4(d) of the platform dealing with 'public health' was further boosted by the passage of the *Tuberculosis Act* 1946.

---

[60] *C.P.D.*, Vol. 185, 3 & 4 October 1945, p.6430.

3 CONSTITUTION ALTERATION INITIATIVES AND LABOR AND THE COAL INDUSTRY

The advances Labor was making in pursuing and enacting the platform were positive. Chifley had actively pursued a diverse range of planks with marked success, however Labor had once again reached a junction where the pursuit of key platform planks would realistically only be possible if Labor pursued amendments to the Constitution. In November 1945 at Labor's 17th Commonwealth Triennial Conference Chifley outlined his Government's plans for social welfare reform in line with the platform in the face of restrictive High Court judgements striking down the party's social services legislation:

> I now refer to the recent decision of the High Court in regard to social benefits. I think that greater acknowledgment should be paid to the Labor Government in regard to social services, as no Government in this country has done so much for social security as the Labor Governments have done – and that goes back to Federation.

Social Services, I believe, are something for which we should fight. I come to the decision of the High Court, and I tell you the present position. The High Court has, in relation to the Pharmaceutical Benefits Act, made an attack on the powers of appropriation of the Commonwealth Parliament. That power has been challenged, and although the judgement of the Court deals only with that Act, it seems fairly clear that nearly all social security legislation, with the exception of the Old Age and invalid pensions, which are specifically provided for under the Constitution, is challenged.

On the question of social services, the Government will have to make sure whether the power is there or not, and the Government will then have to decide whether a referendum should be taken on that particular matter to place it beyond doubt, so as to ensure social benefits being paid.[61]

Conference ratified Chifley's stance on the referendum proposals and unanimously agreed:

That the Federal Government seek an alteration of the Constitution by referendum as early as possible, to enable the Federal Parliament to effectively legislate for the social and economic needs of the nation.[62]

The Conference demanded action for Labor's platform to be implemented via referendum and although Parliament had recessed for the Christmas break, when it resumed in the new year Chifley wasted little time in bringing the referendum proposals to

---

[61] Australian Labor Party, <u>Official Report of Proceedings of the 17th Commonwealth Triennial Conference</u>, Melbourne, 30 November 1945, pp.46-7

[62] <u>ibid.</u>, p.21.

Caucus for approval. On 12 March 1946 Chifley introduced the proposals and Evatt lead the discussion and moved, 'That the following questions be submitted at the same time on election day.'[63] Evatt outlined the proposals as well as providing details of legal opinion that the Government had sought in connection with each referendum proposal:

> 1. Maternity allowances, child endowment, unemployment and sickness benefits, hospital benefits (including private hospitals), widows' pensions, medical and dental services and family allowances.

> 2. Organised marketing of primary products, irrespective of section 92 of the Constitution.

> 3. Terms and conditions of employment in industry.[64]

The referendum proposals were warmly welcomed by Caucus, however there were a few members who had not forgotten Fisher's ill-fated attempt in 1913 to link referendum proposals with elections and Falstein and Conelan unsuccessfully moved to amend Evatt's earlier motion:

> That the Referendum be held on a day prior to Election Day, such day to be fixed by the Cabinet or by the Prime Minister.[65]

There was wide ranging debate in the Caucus room and a number of unsuccessful amendments were proposed in relation to the substance and form of the referendum proposals, however Caucus finally approved that:

---

63 *Caucus Minutes*, 12 March 1946.
64 ibid.
65 ibid.

The referendum proposals be submitted to the people at the forthcoming election, be prepared on the one ballot paper and voted upon separately.[66]

On 27 March Evatt introduced the Constitution Alteration (Social Services) Bill, the Constitution Alteration (Organised Marketing of Primary Products) Bill and the Constitution Alteration (Industrial Employment) Bill into the House. Labor's social reform agenda, based on the platform, had been threatened by the High Court judgement in the *Pharmaceutical Benefits Case* and Labor now moved to consolidate its power to enact social reform measures by amending the Constitution. Labor were determined to pursue the platform even if this meant confronting the onerous task of submitting its proposals to a referendum and Evatt outlined the rationale for the Social Services Bill:

> Ever since federation, it has been assumed by successive governments and parliaments that the National Parliament could spend for any all Australian purpose the money that it raises. In 1944, I warned the House and the country that, under the Constitution as it stands, the legal foundations for even the most urgent modern social service legislation were doubtful and insecure. The High Court's decision last year in the pharmaceuticals benefits' case has shown that these doubts were only too well founded. The object of this Bill is to place Australian social service legislation on a sound legal footing.[67]

The Government had also attempted to enact plank 11 of its 'Economic' section of the platform with respect to introducing 'Australian wide cooperative pools for the marketing and financing of farm products',[68] and Labor now took the opportunity to

---

[66] ibid.
[67] *C.P.D.*, Vol. 186, 27 March 1946, pp.646-7.

effectively deal with the organised marketing of Australia's primary products by submitting a proposal to the people:

> With the exception of the war years, attempts by this Parliament to give effective assistance to primary producers by organising the marketing of primary products have encountered two constitutional difficulties. One is the fact that while the Parliament may make laws with respect only to trade and commerce with other countries and among the states, it may not make laws with respect to trade and commerce within a single state. The second difficulty is the requirement laid down in section 92 of the Constitution, that trade, commerce and intercourse among the States shall be "absolutely free". The present Bill is designed to obviate both these difficulties.
>
> … The marketing of primary products has ramifications which are Australian wide, and the national interest demands that the Commonwealth should be free to take measures to regulate marketing in a manner that will serve not only the interests of producers but also those of the people of Australia as a whole. [69]

The third Bill Labor proposed covered the area of industrial employment and sought to provide the Government with the power to regulate, either directly or indirectly, the terms and conditions of employment in industry, thus providing the Government with the means to effectively pursue over twenty sub-planks of section 10 of the platform dealing with 'Industrial Regulation'[70]:

---

[68] Australian Labor Party, <u>Official Report of Proceedings of the 17th Commonwealth Triennial Conference</u>, Melbourne, 30 November 1945, p.7.

[69] *C.P.D.*, Vol. 186, 27 March 1946, pp.650-1.

[70] See: Australian Labor Party, <u>Official Report of Proceedings of the 17th Commonwealth Triennial Conference</u>, Melbourne, 30 November 1945, section

During the war years, the defence power of the Commonwealth enabled this Parliament, and under its authority, the Government, not only to improve and extend the existing machinery for conciliation and arbitration but also to deal directly, as occasion required, with almost every phase of the terms and conditions of employment. Wages, hours, holidays, and working conditions were regulated.

... The most important aspect of this Bill, is the positive powers it will confer. It will enable this Parliament to fix standard hours in any industry, though not in occupations that are not industrial in character, in accordance with the distinction between industrial and other types of employment drawn by the decisions of the High Court under section 51 (xxxv). It will enable disputes to be arbitrated upon if they are industrial in character. Employment of many types does not fall within that category. It will enable this Parliament to fix the basic wage ... [the] maximum weekly hours of labour that may be worked in industry throughout the Commonwealth ... In short, the Bill will enable this Australian Parliament to discharge all the normal responsibilities of government in an advanced industrial democracy. [71]

All three referendum proposals had the total support of Caucus and the wider labour movement, and provided a blueprint of the Government's plans to amend the Constitution to ostensibly provide it with increased legal coverage to enact planks of the platform without having to run the gauntlet of challenges in the High Court. The legislation was passed through the Parliament and the three Constitution Alteration Acts were now placed on the

---

10, pp.7-8.
[71] *C.P.D.*, Vol. 186, 27 March 1946, pp.651-3.

notice paper in preparation for their submission to the Australian people at the next federal election.

Nationalisation of Wireless Transmission

The pursuit of constitutional change by Labor did not hamper its drive to enact other planks of the platform and in June the Government moved to nationalise Australia's overseas telecommunications services in line with part of plank 4(e) of the platform that provided for the 'Nationalisation of wireless transmission, including broadcasting'. On 20 June, Calwell outlined the purpose of the Bill to the House:

> It deals with the transfer to national ownership of the external telecommunications services now owned and operated by Amalgamated Wireless Australasia Limited and the establishment of a statutory corporation to operate both radio and cable services linking Australia with other countries. This Bill is one of a number of similar pieces of legislation which will be enacted by the parliaments of all self-governing countries in the British Commonwealth and Empire.[72]

The nationalisation of overseas telecommunications was an important measure with respect of the platform and it was soon followed by legislation to enact plank 10(p) of the Industrial Regulations section platform that called for a 'Commonwealth Mines and Regulation Act'.[73]

Labor and the Coal Industry

---

[72] *C.P.D.*, Vol. 187, 20 June 1946, pp.1653-4.
[73] Australian Labor Party, <u>Official Report of Proceedings of the 17th Commonwealth Triennial Conference</u>, Melbourne, 26 November 1945, p.6.

Labor first introduced the plank at the 6th Commonwealth Conference in 1915 when a motion was successfully moved on behalf of the Australian Labour Federation of Western Australia, to incorporate a plank into the federal platform for a specific Commonwealth Mine Regulation Act to be introduced to handle/deal with issues surrounding mining.[74] The Government had moved during the war to control the coal industry through the defence power and with the conclusion of the war it now sought to strengthen its level of control over the operations of the coal industry in line with plank 10(p) of the platform. The Government's actions were also predicated on industrial action in the industry and its impact on the country. In September 1945 coal miners, steel miners and waterside workers were involved in industrial action that virtually crippled the nation, with power and gas having to be rationed by the Government. The war had ended and communist influence in the labour movement had increased as communists began to contest union elections and assert their dominance in industrial campaigns. This dominance had come to the fore during the campaign with the coal and steel miners and the waterside workers where militant communist led unionists literally did battle against the moderate right wing unions to see who would control the sector. The Official paper of the Communist Party in Australia, the *Tribune* provided commentary at the conclusion of the dispute in December:

> The aim of the BHP monopoly and the right wing traitors in the Labor Movement to crush the Ironworkers' Union has now definitely failed … The smashing of the Ironworkers' Union would have paved the way for a general offensive against the workers. This conspiracy was defeated by the magnificent fighting spirit of the striking

---

[74] Australian Labor Party, <u>Official Report of the Sixth Commonwealth Conference of the Australian Labor Party</u>, Adelaide, 4 June 1915, p.46.

ironworkers and the generous aid rendered by the miners, seamen and F.E.D.F.A. members. These are outstanding and permanent gains which have been won for the working class. The miners have reached agreement with the Governments on their 'Five Year Plan' ... Had they [BHP and the ALP right wing] succeeded in smashing the ironworkers, it would have undermined the position of every union and paved the way for a general drive by the employing class against the living standards of the working class.[75]

The strike was settled by arbitration, however it sent a clear signal to the Government of the importance of ensuring that industrial harmony be maintained in the coal industry, especially in New South Wales where eighty percent of the nation's coal was produced. Labor had depended on the defence power for the validity of the *Coal Production (War-time) Act* 1944 and the *Coal Mines Profits (War Time) Act* 1944, however the end of the war also meant that the defence power Labor relied on would gradually become redundant, so the Government moved to consolidate their position with respect of the coal industry as well as enacting plank 10(p) of the platform and on 24 July Dedman outlined the Bill to the House:

Today in the midst of the transition from war to civil production, we are confronted with a dangerously low level of coal stocks on the one hand and an ever-mounting demand on the other ... During the war years, we had to improvise and patch as best we could in the circumstances ... Today, however, we face a peace period in which the Government is determined that we shall proceed vigorously on a program of basic re-organisation. That is why we

---

[75]*Tribune*, Sydney, 18 December 1945.

mark the first year of peace by bringing down this legislation to lay the framework for a new deal for the New South Wales industry, which produces over 80% of our black coal ... This Government, and the Government of New South Wales, must make a fresh start at resolving the clearly recognisable problems of discontent and under production in the industry. Only a wide, systematic and thorough re-organisation of the industry will meet the real needs.[76]

The Bill was supported by the union, however the Northern Colliery Proprietors' Association were less than complimentary. Wells for the union stated:

The Bill does not nationalise the industry. Instead, it brings the industry under a measure of control ... The owners fought the Bill, but that was just a big piece of bluff. The Coal Board will reorganise the industry, provide loans for better equipment and more efficient working of mines and guarantee a reasonable profit. Research stations will be established and everything else done to bring the industry to the highest level.[77]

Forster for Northern Colliery Proprietors' Association was of the opinion that:

So long as the Prime Minister (Mr Chifley) retains control of the coalmining industry, as he does under this Bill, then we say he will not get one extra ton of coal, because it is an invitation to the Miners' Federation to do its collective bargaining direct with the head of the Government, thereby disregarding the employers, special tribunals and

---

[76] *C.P.D.*, Vol. 188, 24 July 1946, pp.3007-8.
[77] *Newcastle Morning Herald*, 2 September 1946

the Arbitration Court. [78]

The Bill was passed despite the rumblings of the Northern Colliery Proprietors' Association and it consolidated the Government's continued control over the industry in line with plank 10(p) of the platform. The Coal Industry was important to the economic wellbeing of Australia and although the continued mining of the resource was important, so too was the ability to transport it and other goods around the country.

National Rail Standardisation

The deficiencies in the Australian rail transport system were highlighted during the war and Labor now moved to rectify the problems experienced during the conflict and in the process sought to enact two planks of the platform. Plank 3(f) of the 'Methods' section outlined that Labor was, 'to vest the Commonwealth Parliament with authority to proceed with the Royal Commission scheme of unification of railway gauges, provided the Commonwealth make the necessary monetary provision'[79] and plank (c) of the 'National Credit' area contained in the 'Progressive Reforms' section of the platform that called for a 'Plan to extend Australian secondary industries to secure a maximum of industrial self-sufficiency, and to provide for effective transport services for the nation'.[80] On 2 August 1946, Ward, Minister for Transport provided a brief history of the Australian rail transport system to the House when he introduced the Railway Standardisation Agreement Bill:

> Since the first railway was built in Australia, in 1854, the
> growth of Australian railways has not progressed according

---

[78] *Newcastle Morning Herald*, 26 July 1946

[79] Australian Labor Party, <u>Official Report of Proceedings of the 16th Commonwealth Conference</u>, Sydney, 16 December 1943, p.3.

[80] <u>ibid</u>., p.5.

to any national plan, and state boundaries have accentuated the difficulties arising out of any national railway policy …The difficulties of interstate rail transport have been apparent for many years … In Australia, we suffered a serious handicap in the transport of men and war materials because there are fifteen break-of-gauge points in our railway system … One of the most important aspects of standardisation of railways is that it will permit the standardisation of trucks, locomotives, and other railway equipment. [81]

Ward then outlined the objectives of the Bill and what Labor hoped to achieve:

After a full examination of the facts, the Commonwealth Government has come to the conclusion that the standardisation and modernisation of our railway systems is an essential defence work. Whilst the project is advanced by the Commonwealth primarily as being necessary for defence purposes, it cannot be overlooked that the economic gains resultant from the adoption of uniformity in gauges and railway equipment, would be tremendous.[82]

Standardisation of railways, coupled with modernisation, will enable the number of types of locomotives, passenger rolling stock and goods vehicles, to be reduced considerably.

Advantages to defence and civilian traffic may be briefly summarised: Standardisation will obviate the necessity for changing trains at present break of gauge points, thus eliminating delay in the transfer of passengers and goods, as

---

[81] *C.P.D.*, Vol.187, 2 August 1946, p.3625-6.
[82] ibid., p.3629.

well as the labour involved therein; and enable rolling stock to be used on all lines, which would:

1. Allow of the most economical use of the available rolling stock, by using it for through journeys, thus avoiding congestion, and sometimes empty back-running from break-of-gauge points.

2. Facilitate repair and replacement, since all railway work-shops, foundries &c. in the several States would use standard parts. Repair and replacement of rolling stock would be speedier, and less liable to interruption by enemy attack, owing to the wide dispersal of the workshops.

3. Facilitate the marshalling of trains for strategic and tactical moves, as a result of the interchangeability of rolling stock.

4. Allow of the employment of standard trains in all States for service purposes, thus facilitating staff work and administration generally.[83]

The Bill was passed in line with the relevant planks of the platform and provided for an agreement between the Commonwealth, Victoria, South Australia and New South Wales to carry out the necessary work to convert the broad gauge lines of Victorian and South Australia to the standard gauge lines of New South Wales. The Railways Standardisation Bill was also the last piece of legislation based on the platform introduced by the Government before it went to a federal election in September 1946.[84][85]

---

[83] ibid.

[84] In 1949 the Government also passed the *Railway Standardisation (South Australia) Agreement Act* 1949 to strengthen the initial agreement between the Commonwealth and South Australia.

45

4 THE 1946 FEDERAL ELECTION AND THE PASSAGE OF THE SOCIAL SERVICES REFERENDUM

The Government had shown its supporters that it could govern during the war, it was now governing in the peace and implementing stated policy goals in line with the platform. On 28 September 1946 Australia went to the polls and the Chifley Government was returned with a majority in both the House of Representatives and the Senate. Labor won forty-three seats in the House, losing six from the last election. The biggest blow to the government was the loss of Forde in his seat of Capricornia, where he was defeated by the Country Party. However, the biggest surprise was in the Senate where Labor won five out of the six states which meant that from 1 July 1947 it would have thirty-three Senators out of a total of thirty-six in the chamber.

The election result was a triumph for Chifley who had ensured that the wartime government was returned to office, unlike his British counterpart Churchill who was defeated at the polls at the war's end. The result was a rare achievement despite the fact that some in the mainstream press regarded it as rather pedestrian:

> In the midst of a world still partly darkened by shadows cast from the past, and while other people's tread uncertainly their paths of political evolution, Australia has displayed a steadiness of political outlook which deserves to be emulated ... The victory of the Chifley Government is probably due to more than one factor. Obviously, the Australian people regard the Labour Government's service during the last three years as having entitled it to a further term in charge of Commonwealth administration. This is the main factor that has actuated electors in their voting, but it is allied with other reasons. Whatever inclination there was for electors to be attracted by the policies of other parties – and there is no doubt that up to the last minute, this attraction had been substantial – when the testing time came electors were not prepared to take the risk.[86]

The new Labor ministry under Chifley was decidedly different from the ministry that first took up the reins in 1941. Curtin had passed away, Forde and Froste had lost their seats, Beasley was High Commissioner in London and Makin was Minister in Washington, whilst Senators Collings and Fraser and Lazzarini were not re-elected by Caucus. The party political changes in the aftermath of the election were significant, however of even greater significance was the fact that Labor had also submitted the three Referendum proposals to the people and for the first time in the history of a Federal Labor Government, a referendum proposal was successful as outlined in Table 3. Labor's electoral success was enhanced by the passage of the 'Social Services' referendum with almost 55% of Australians voting in favour of the proposal together with the support of all six states. Labor's social services referendum

---

[86] *Canberra Times*, 30 September 1946.

was carried in every state with an overwhelming mandate and the Party now had the opportunity to advance the social reform planks in the platform. Labor's joy at the passage of the 'Social Services' referendum was tempered somewhat by the fact that the remaining two proposals came agonisingly close to also being passed, as can be seen in Table 3 below.

Table 1 – 1946 Referendum Results

Subject	Yes Voters - States	Yes Voters – % Of Total	Carried Or Lost
Maternity allowances, child endowment, unemployment and sickness benefits, hospital benefits (including private hospitals), widows' pensions, medical and dental services and family allowances	New South Wales, Western Australia, South Australia, Victoria, Tasmania, Queensland	54.39	Carried
Organised marketing of primary products, irrespective of section 92 of the Constitution	New South Wales, Western Australia, Victoria	50.57	Lost
Terms and conditions of employment in industry	New South Wales, Western Australia, Victoria	50.20	Lost

As Table 1 shows, the marketing of primary products proposal that sought to provide Labor with the power to enact plank 11 of the 'Economic' section of the platform with respect of introducing 'Australian wide cooperative pools for the marketing and financing of farm products' was approved by 50.57% of Australians, whilst the proposal dealing with terms and conditions of employment for

Australian workers that would have provided Labor with the opportunity to pursue over twenty sub-planks of section 10 of the platform dealing with 'Industrial Regulation' was approved by 50.20% of voters. The result on this basis really was a major achievement for the Government, as all three proposals were endorsed by a majority of voters. However, unfortunately for Labor the marketing and industrial arbitration proposals were only supported by three States, with South Australia, Queensland and Tasmania voting against the proposals. A majority of Australians had signaled their intention that they wanted the Federal Government to have power over the marketing of primary products and industrial employment, ironically however it was the Constitution that thwarted the majority vote becoming law. Labor had once again fallen short of achieving its objectives of pursuing and enacting key platform planks because of the vagaries of the Constitution through the provisions of the Constitution. Labor was extremely unlucky, of the nineteen referendum proposals introduced since federation (three being carried) up until that time, only one other had received a majority of votes but was defeated.[87] In the last session of the year Labor passed the Constitution Alteration (Social Services) Act 1946 and the referendum proposal was enacted into law and Labor now had the opportunity to advance the social reform planks in the platform.

The election and referendum results provided Labor with a clear mandate to govern and an opportunity to continue to pursue major policy initiatives based on the platform. Chifley's Government had shown the Australian people that it could govern in a time of crisis, now it had an opportunity to put its post war policies to the test. Labor went to the Christmas break with a renewed sense of purpose and vigour unaware that the 1947

---

[87] On 6 March 1937 the Lyons Government sought a referendum on 'Air Navigation'. The proposal received 54.39% of the total vote but was only carried in two states, Victoria and Queensland.

session would become one of the most controversial in the history of the Federal Parliament.

The Governor General, Industrial Relations and Estate Duties

Labor hit the ground running after the election enacting a number of important platform planks. In January 1947, Chifley set the tone for the new government when he announced the nomination of William McKell as Governor General thus enacting plank 30 of the 'Electoral and Constitutional' section of the platform that called on Labor to establish the precedent of, 'appointing an Australian citizen to the position of Governor General shall be followed should Labor be in power when the position falls vacant'.[88]

Chifley wanted an Australian Governor General 'without the pomp and plumes and social glitter'[89] generally associated with the position and he wanted the Governor General to be a 'man of the people'[90] and somebody all Australian's could relate to and respect. The choice of McKell in line with the platform caused uproar on the conservative side of politics with Menzies leading the charge:

> It constitutes the most deplorable incident in the Government's growing record of political jobbery. One is forced to the conclusion that it is expressly designed to lower the Governor-Generalship in significance and esteem, and so weaken our vital connection with Great Britain and with the British Crown.

The appointment of McKell was soon followed by the introduction of Stevedoring legislation enacting plank 10(g) of the 'Industrial Regulation' section of the platform that called on the party to

---

[88] Australian Labor Party, <u>Official Report of Proceedings of the 17th Commonwealth Triennial Conference</u>, Melbourne, 30 November 1945, p.9.
[89] Kelly, V., <u>A Man of the People</u>. Alpha, Sydney, 1971, p.160.
[90] <u>ibid</u>.

'Repeal the *Transport Workers Act*'.[91] The *Transport Workers Acts* of 1928 and 1929 required waterside workers to be licensed and sought to regulate conditions on the wharves to the detriment of the workers. On 21 February 1946 Evatt introduced the Bill:

> The aim of this Bill is to achieve industrial peace, and continuity and efficiency of work in the stevedoring industry, which is an essential factor in the transport of this country and thus to its economy.[92]

The repeal of the *Transport Workers Act* 1929 had been a long standing plank in the platform that had now been successfully enacted by Labor. A month after the introduction of the Stevedoring Bill Labor moved to enact plank 5 of the 'Taxation and Finance' section of the platform relating to 'Estate duties' calling on Labor to amend:

> The Federal 'Estates Duties Act' to provide for the prevention of evasions of death duties by creation of trust deeds and such like instruments.[93]

On 27 March 1947, Chifley introduced the Estate Duty Assessment Bill into the House to strengthen Estate Duties laws in line with the platform:

> The amendment made by clause 5 relates to the deduction allowable in respect of State and Commonwealth income tax and land tax which become due and payable after death and within one year after payment of duty. The intention of the law was to permit the deduction for income

---

[91] Australian Labor Party, <u>Official Report of Proceedings of the 17th Commonwealth Triennial Conference</u>, Melbourne, 30 November 1945, p.6.
[92] *C.P.D.*, Vol. 190, 21 February 1947, p.123.
[93] Australian Labor Party, <u>Official Report of Proceedings of the 17th Commonwealth Triennial Conference</u>, Melbourne, 30 November 1945, p.5.

tax and land tax assessed subsequent to the date of death on income derived and land owned by the deceased during his lifetime. In many cases however, owing to the complicated nature of the estate a considerable time elapses before the estate duty can be finally assessed … The unintended effect of the present law is that many large estates are, by reason of the unavoidable delay in completing the estate duty assessment, receiving the benefit of very substantial deductions in respect of income tax and land tax assessed on income derived and land owned by the executors subsequent to the death of the deceased. The amendment … will ensure that proper effect shall be given to the original intention of the law.[94]

The original intention of the law would be upheld as well as enacting plank 5 of the 'Taxation and Finance' section of the platform relating to 'Estate duties'. However, whilst stevedoring and estate duties were important policy initiatives delivered by Labor, moves were also made to provide an adequate compensation regime for seamen in line with plank 22(h) of the Navigation section of the platform that called for, 'The compulsory insurance of crews by shipowners against accident or death.'[95]

<u>Navigation and Shipping</u>

On 1 May 1947 Senator Ashley, Minister for Supply and Shipping detailed the Bill to the Senate:

> The Seaman's Compensation Act is an important Commonwealth Act which provides compensation cover for those workers who, while employed on the high seas,

---

[94] *C.P.D.*, Vol. 191, 27 March 1947, pp.1266-7.

[95] Australian Labor Party, <u>Official Report of Proceedings of the 17th Commonwealth Triennial Conference</u>, Melbourne, 30 November 1945, p.6.

are outside the scope of the various state compensation Acts ... Naturally, seamen regard these new provisions as representing the current Commonwealth view of what is fair and reasonable compensation for injuries.[96]

The Bill outlined the benefits a seaman could expect if he was injured, maimed or killed and set out specific payment schedules for these as well as for industrial diseases. In closing Ashley stated:

> I commend the Bill to the Senate, as a measure which will give to seamen a compensation law in keeping with modern conceptions of social justice, and one which their services to the nation have richly earned.[97]

The coverage provided to seamen by Labor was extensive and brought it into line with general Commonwealth insurance practices and whilst the platform related to the provision of insurance by shipowners this did not stop Labor taking the initiative to ensure that workers, in this instance 'seamen', were adequately covered in case of accident or worse. The social policy initiatives continued to be pursued by the Government and following the passage of the *Constitution Alteration (Social Services) Act 1946*, Chifley officially moved to ensure that Labor's Social Policy platform initiatives were provided with a secure legal foundation. On 15 May 1947 the Government introduced the Social Services Legislation Declaratory Bill into the Parliament. Senator McKenna, Minister for Health and Minister for Social Services, outlined the rationale for the Bill:

> The purpose of the Bill is to make use of the new powers vested in the Parliament as a result of the recent referendum to place on a firm legal foundation certain

---

[96] *C.P.D.*, Vol. 191, 1 May 1947, pp.1791-2.
[97] <u>ibid</u>., pp.1792-3.

existing legislation of a social services character ... The constitutional position in regard to our social services legislation ... [and] the only specific power to enact such legislation which the Parliament had was to provide invalid and old age pensions ... The decision of the High Court in the Pharmaceutical Benefits Act case showed, however that the appropriation power could only be exercised for those purposes which are stated or implied elsewhere in the Constitution, and that Parliament had been acting on too wide a view of its power.[98]

Senator McKenna outlined the form and scope of the legislation with respect to the social policy planks of the platform that the Bill would legitimise:

The new power which now resides in the Parliament is to make laws with respect to the provision of maternity allowances, widows' pensions, child endowment, unemployment, pharmaceutical, sickness and hospital benefits, medical and dental services – but not so as to authorise any form of civil conscription – benefits to students and family allowances. The view of the Government's legal advisers is ... that the Commonwealth cannot rely on these new powers to support legislation enacted before 19 December 1946 unless that legislation has been confirmed by Parliament on or after that date ... The Bill, if passed, will ensure their validity by declaring them to have full force and effect.[99]

The Social Services Declaratory legislation was strengthened by similar legislation in 1948.[100] The effect of the legislation providing

---

[98] *C.P.D.*, Vol. 191, 15 May 1947, p.2392.
[99] ibid., p.2393.
[100] *Social Services Declaratory Act* 1948

legitimacy to key planks of the Social Reform section of the platform, plank 17 – An adequate Housing Scheme; plank 18 – Widows' and Children's Pensions; and plank 20 – Motherhood and Childhood Endowment.

Public Health

The 'Public Health' plank contained in section 4(d) of the platform was also strengthened by the fact that the Parliament could now legitimately legislate for pharmaceutical, sickness and hospital benefits and medical and dental services. The referendum result was crucial to Labor maintaining and pursuing a viable social reform agenda based on the platform and it wasted little time introducing legislation to provide free medicine to the people of Australia and on 30 May 1947 sought leave to introduce the Pharmaceutical Benefits Bill.[101]   In response to Opposition questions on the Bill, Senator McKenna outlined the rationale for the legislation:

> ... the basic principles which underlay the Pharmaceutical Benefits Acts of 1944 and 1945 have not been changed in this measure ... The Government feels that it is under an obligation of good faith to the people of this country to fulfil its promise and to implement the pharmaceutical benefits scheme as early as possible. The scheme is merely a modification of the original one.[102]

The *Pharmaceutical Benefits Act* 1947 was passed in the Parliament, however the Australian branch of the British Medical Association (BMA) resisted any attempts to cooperate in any schemes associated with the legislation. The BMA also made its position on the Act clear to Labor:

---

[101] *C.P.D.*, Vol. 192, 30 May 1947, p.3198.
[102] *C.P.D.*, Vol 192, 4 June 1947, p.3319.

Principles enunciated by the British Medical Association are: (i) Opposition to a full time salaried service. (ii) Freedom from control in professional matters. (iii) Freedom for the patient to choose his own doctor. (iv) Freedom of the Doctor to practise where and in the way he thinks best. (v) Adequate medical representation on controlling bodies. (vi) Freedom from political interference. (vii) A stable guaranteed fund to finance the service.[103]

The Australian Federal Council of the BMA also outlined to Senator McKenna the major issues the BMA had with Labor's planned pharmaceutical scheme:

1. The principle of discrimination as to their entitlement to pharmaceutical benefits between those members of the public whose requirements come within the limits of the formulary and those whose requirements are not so covered. It is this principle which involves an interference with the doctor's freedom of judgement in prescribing for his patient.

2. The principle of penal clauses, whereby a doctor who voluntarily uses the government forms and formulary finds himself not only restricted in his choice of the treatment which he may order for his patient, and the subject to the intervention of a third party in the transaction, but also finds himself liable to heavy penalties if his procedure varies from that laid down by the Government.

3. The principle of control by a government department rather than by a corporate body.

---

[103] *Medical Journal of Australia*, Sydney, 14 February 1948, p.212.

4. The opportunity provided for the introduction of a nationalised medical service by means of an act not drawn up for that purpose.[104]

Chifley labelled the leaders of the BMA as 'conservative shellbacks' for their stance on the issue,[105] however this did not stop the BMA commencing a court challenge against the validity of the Act or of informing Australian doctors how to destroy the scheme:

> The Federal Council of the British Medical Association in Australia desires each member of the Association to know the actual steps to be taken in the event of the Pharmaceutical Benefits Act 1947, coming into operation.

Each member should:

i. Return to the Association Branch Office prescription forms and Formulary sent by the controlling authority under the Act.

ii. Continue to prescribe as heretofore on private forms or lodge prescription books.

iii. Ensure that all patients receive a copy of the printed statement sent by his own Branch of the British Medical Association.[106]

The BMA's attacks on the scheme both from the medical profession and through the courts saw the matter eventually proceed to the High Court[107] where in a split 3-2 decision[108] the

---

[104] *Medical Journal of Australia*, Sydney, 17 April 1948, p.513.

[105] Sawer, op cit., p.198.

[106] *Medical Journal of Australia*, Sydney, 1 May 1948, p.568.

[107] *British Medical Association v Commonwealth* (August-October 1949) 79 C.L.R. 201

[108] Latham C.J., Rich, Williams and Webb JJ held that the free medical scheme was invalid whilst McTiernan and Dixon JJ dissented.

Court invalidated the scheme on the ground that the compulsory use of Commonwealth prescription forms for medicines within the federal formulary contained in *the Pharmaceutical Benefits Act* 1947 constituted 'civil conscription' within the meaning of the new section 51(xxiiA) of the Constitution which was passed in the 1946 referendum. The High Court had again shown a preparedness to interpret the constitution narrowly when Labor was in power pursuing its policy platform. This theme was touched on by McMullin who stated:

> From Labor's viewpoint the court had displayed since its inception a disconcerting tendency to reserve its most restrictive interpretations of the national government's constitutional powers for the times when the Federal Parliamentary Labor Party was ascendant.[109]

The adverse decision was a setback to Labor's program to legislate for plank 4(d) of the platform calling for the 'Nationalisation of public health', however this did not stop the Government pursuing other core planks of the platform despite the increasing threat of legislation running the gauntlet of restrictive interpretations from the bench of the High Court: the battle for the banks was about to commence.

---

[109] McMullin, 1991, <u>op cit.</u>, p.246.

5 THE COMMONWEALTH BANK

In May 1947 the Government commenced the operation of section 48 of the *Banking Act* 1945 that effectively precluded State Governments, State Instrumentalities and local government authorities from dealing with any private banking institution.[110] At the end of May the Melbourne City Council launched legal proceedings against the constitutional validity of section 48 of the *Banking Act* 1945.[111] The *State Banking Case* proceeded to the High Court where on 13 August 1947 the High Court determined, by a majority decision of five to one, that the operation of section 48 was *ultra vires*. The High Court's decision was not unexpected, however *obiter* comments by some of the justices indicated that Labor's banking legislation could be threatened by future court challenges against the operation of the banking legislation, and given the political orthodoxy of the bench it would more than likely be ruled *ultra vires*. The High Court's decision and interpretation of

---

[110] This measure precluded over 200 local government authorities from banking in the private sector.
[111] *City of Melbourne v Commonwealth (The State Banking Case)* (July-August 1947) 74 C.L.R. 31.

the statute was a blow to Labor, however Chifley was undaunted and as Crisp states:

> Chifley had let it be known quietly in an appropriate quarter that if the private banks sought to emasculate essential provisions of the 1945 Acts, on whatever pretext or behind whatever 'front', he would go to the limit to sustain the basic purposes of that legislation.[112]

On 14 August, a day after the decision Chifley discussed the legal implications of the decision with Evatt and McKenna as well as with the Governor of the Commonwealth Bank and the Bank's senior Officers. On 16 August Cabinet met to discuss the *State Banking Case* and with Evatt and McKenna already aware of what was to come, Chifley dropped his bombshell. Evatt provided Cabinet with an overview of the ramifications of the decision and then Chifley outlined the choices available to them:

> The Government could either swallow the decision and await an attack by the private banks on the vital sections of the 1945 Acts, or they could remove the challengers by nationalising the banks.[113]

Chifley's statement did not come as a shock to either Evatt or McKenna, however they noted that after the announcement there was 'complete stunned shock'[114] by members, then, after the gravity of what Chifley proposed had sunk in, there was 'a good deal of jubilation'.[115] Chifley asked every Cabinet member present[116] for their personal opinion on the appropriate course of action, and

---

[112] Crisp, 1977, op cit., pp.324-5.
[113] ibid., p.327.
[114] ibid.
[115] ibid.
[116] Dedman, Calwell and Ward were overseas when Chifley discussed the nationalisation of the Banks with Cabinet.

to a man they asserted that the appropriate course of action for Labor was to nationalise the banks in line with plank 4(a) of the platform. When Cabinet had provided unanimous support for the nationalisation proposal Chifley then provided his response:

> '*Well that's the decision then*', he said.

> To which Pollard interjected, '*Wait a minute, what about you Chif – where do you stand?*'

> Chifley replied, '*With you and the boys, Reggie, to the last ditch.*'[117]

Chifley's decision to pursue plank 4(a) of the platform to nationalise the banks has been criticised for being somewhat rash, with Sawer stating:

> It was policy conceived in pique, and its execution was bound to be blundering since an operation of that size, directed against such powerful and ably-defended adversaries, required long

Sawer and others who take the view that Chifley's actions were based on a 'fit of pique' have underestimated Chifley's decision making abilities and with a decision of this magnitude it would not have been taken lightly or arrived at in a 'fit of pique'. In his biography on Chifley, Crisp touched on the episode stating:

> Unlike most people, Chifley *lived* for politics and government and he gave practically his whole time and thought to them. The charges that his decisions – to nationalise in 1947 (three days after the Melbourne City Council Case verdict), to appeal to the Privy Council in 1948 (two days after the nationalisation verdict), and after

---

[117] McMullin, 1991, <u>op cit.</u>, p.246.

the Privy Council decision in 1949 to give the banks 'virile competition' through the Commonwealth Bank – were all taken suddenly and out of pique displays a complete ignorance of the thought Chifley gave in advance to possible future contingencies and the ways in which they should be tackled. This advance planning was a habit which never ceased to impress his close collaborators.[118]

Chifley and Cabinet had unanimously endorsed the pursuit of section 4(a) of the Platform calling for the 'Nationalisation of Banking', a plank that was first approved by Federal Conference in 1919 and which was a core plank of the platform. At the conclusion of the meeting, members dispersed for lunch and when he left the room Chifley was approached by journalists inquiring about any news of Cabinet decisions, to which Chifley informed them:

> Oh, Don [Rogers, his press secretary] may have a little piece in there that'll interest you.[119]

The 'little piece' of interest Chifley alluded to stated:

> Cabinet today authorised the Attorney General (Dr Evatt) and myself to prepare legislation for submission to the Federal Parliamentary Labor Party for the nationalisation of banking, other than State banks, with proper protection for shareholders, depositors, borrowers and staff of private banks.[120]

In what has become folklore, it was said that a senior press correspondent bit through the stem of his pipe when he read the statement and realised what was being proposed. The veracity or

---

[118] see footnote 7 in Crisp, 1977, op cit., p.331
[119] ibid., p.328.
120 ibid., p.328.

otherwise of this actually happening is a moot point, however it highlighted the magnitude of the task that Labor had set itself in enacting the platform on this issue. Chifley's announcement was made whilst Parliament was in recess and it was not until 16 September 1947, almost a month after the announcement, that Caucus met to discuss Cabinet's decision. At the Caucus meeting Chifley asked leave to introduce a Bill for the nationalisation of banking stating:

> There was a recommendation from Cabinet for the nationalisation of banking and he moved for its adoption.[121]

Caucus unanimously supported the proposal despite the fact that members had to wait a month to officially endorse it. However, the forces arrayed against the proposal, notably the Opposition and the banking sector, wasted no time in launching a full scale blitzkrieg against the proposal almost immediately after it was announced on the 16th August, so that when Caucus met to discuss the proposal there was already a concerted and well-orchestrated campaign to destroy it. The proposal polarised political and public opinion with Duthie poignantly observing that, 'all hell broke loose',[122] after the announcement and Labor battened down the hatches to ride out the political storm.

On 15 October 1947 Chifley introduced the Banking Bill into the Parliament for the first reading and a division was called by the Opposition.[123] The intent of the Opposition to stall the passage of the Bill at every opportunity was clear, however this did not stop Chifley outlining the scope and form of the legislation to enact plank 4(a) of the platform in his second reading stating:

---

[121] *Caucus Minutes*, 16 September 1947.

[122] Duthie, G., <u>I Had 50,000 Bosses: Memoirs of a Labor Backbencher 1946-1975.</u>. Angus & Robertson, Sydney, 1984, p.42.

[123] Labor won the division on the numbers by 42 to 27, see; *C.P.D.*, Vol. 193, 15 October 1947, p.796.

The purpose of this Bill is to empower the Commonwealth Bank to take over the banking business at present conducted in Australia by private banks. State banks and savings banks will not be affected.

It will be the responsibility of the Commonwealth Bank under this legislation:

(a)   To provide, in accordance with the conditions of normal banking business, adequate banking facilities for any state or person requiring them;

(b)   To conduct its business without discrimination; and

(c)   To observe, except as otherwise required by law, the practices and usages customary among bankers and, in particular, to maintain strict secrecy within the law as to the affairs and dealings of its customers.

The Bill also envisages the development, under public ownership, of a comprehensive banking service that will strengthen and assist the growth of the Australian economy and provide facilities adequate to its rapidly expanding and changing needs.[124]

Chifley expanded on the modern policy of banking in Australia and then turned his attention towards what he described as the 'Labor view of banking':

The Labor Party has maintained for many years that, since the influence of money is so great, the entire monetary and banking system should be controlled by public authorities

---

[124] ibid., p.798.

responsible through the government and parliament to the nation ... Labor policy on banking has envisaged that, together with the elimination of private banking, the Commonwealth Bank would be strengthened to give it adequate control of monetary and credit conditions within Australia and its services would be extended to meet the needs of all sections of the people.[125]

The constitutional issues were central to the introduction of the legislation and after discussing Labor's record with the banks during the war years and the experience gained through the passage of the 1945 Banking legislation Chifley then focused on the constitutional aspects of the Bill:

> The Banking Act of 1945 was framed on the best constitutional advice and the Government felt confident that it would withstand any legal challenge that might be directed against it.

> For example, it seemed quite clear that Parliament had made a law with respect to banking, and had thus acted within the scope of the powers conferred by section 51(xiii) of the constitution, when it enacted section 48 of the Banking Act ... When challenged in the High Court, however section 48 was held to be invalid on the grounds that so long as private banks existed States and State authorities could not be denied the use of their facilities. The decision showed that full public control of banking as sought under the 1945 legislation could not be secured without public ownership of banking. The decision forced the government to re-examine all circumstances, constitutional and otherwise, surrounding the legislation of 1945.

---

[125] ibid., pp.798-9.

> The structure of banking based upon the legislation of 1945 went part of the way towards the objectives which the Labor Party has long advocated in regard to banking ... That position was never accepted without reservation by the private banks and now that the legal foundations of the system have been challenged the Government has decided to proceed with its long standing policy of full public ownership.[126]

In concluding his speech, Chifley castigated opponents who had been attacking the proposals, but he stuck to the core theme of the Bill:

> The proposal to take over the banks is being condemned in some quarters in recklessly extravagant terms; all kinds of hidden purposes are being wrongly ascribed to it from the same sources. The simple truth is this – the reasons and motives for this measure and the uses to which it can and will be applied are no more and no less than I have stated ... Full public ownership of the banks will ensure control of banking in the public interest.[127]

On 23 October 1947, a week after Chifley's second reading speech, Menzies led the attack on the legislation in the Parliament:

> This Bill makes revolutionary changes. It will, of course, by weight of numbers, be passed, but it will be passed without mandate and ... I assert, without popular approval ... If we want to get the real historical foundation of this Bill that is before Parliament and the people tonight we must go back to Karl Marx and the Communist Manifesto.

---

[126] ibid., pp.801-3.
[127] ibid., p.809.

> … Let nobody suppose that these aspiring dictators [Labor] will rest content with the destruction of the banks. That is merely the first giant stride towards complete socialisation, which is to come partly by the ruthless exercise of such powers as the Commonwealth possesses and partly by close collaboration with socialist governments in the States, producing interlocking legislation and the establishment of government trading corporations with monopolistic powers. [128]

Anthony for the Opposition (Country Party) made Menzies' speech look pedestrian:

> This Banking Bill, which the Minister so ardently supports, is the first step in a sinister scheme under which not one farmer but every one of the 250,000 farmers of Australia will ultimately be dispossessed of their farms and 'liquidated' … just as was done in Russia under socialisation twenty years ago … They [Labor] have to conceal the fact that they are implementing a policy designed by the Bolshevik Communists, the worst and most poisonous faction of all the Communist factions. [129]

The speeches by the Opposition mirrored the propaganda war that had been waged by the Opposition and its allies since the first announcement of the measure in August. Labor was besieged by a well-orchestrated daily campaign by the banks and business. The propaganda campaign was intensive and unrelenting, however Chifley's commitment to enacting plank 4(a) of the platform was commendable, however as Crisp noted:

> Chifley was realistic enough to know that with the limited

---

[128] *C.P.D.*, Vol. 194, 23 October 1947, pp.1279-83.
[129] ibid., pp.1302-3.

channels which would be open to Labor, and its very limited funds, even their largest scale efforts would be puny in the existing atmosphere alongside what the banks were doing. "Well, I don't know", he said, "but I wouldn't take a rowing boat out in a storm".[130]

Chifley's analogy was apt, however the storm did not abate and even as the Bill passed through the Parliament a legal challenge was being prepared to kill it.[131] The *Bank Nationalisation Case*, as it became known, reached the High Court on 9 February 1948. Evatt led the Defence for Labor and Barwick headed the challenge for the banks. Barwick took 7 days to outline the case for the Banks, whilst Evatt took an incredible 18 days to outline Labor's defence. On 11 August 1948, some four months after the case commenced, the Court handed down their judgement:

> ... and revealed that once again Barwick's view of section 92 of the constitution had prevailed over what was commonly regarded as good sense and sound law in the form of Evatt's alternative interpretation, which had underpinned the Doc's own 1930s judgements and was to be upheld by a later generation of High Court judges.[132]

Chifley was unperturbed by the ruling of the High Court, and although somewhat disappointed in the decision, he knew that the Court would strike it down, and in a personal note to a friend after the ruling he stated:

> The decision of the High Court was not, of course, unexpected by our people, although I am afraid their [presumably, the judges'] judgement was not based in some

---

[130] Crisp, 1977, op cit., p.333.
[131] *Bank of New South Wales v Commonwealth* (February-August 1948) 76 C.L.R. 1
[132] McMullin, 1991, op cit., p.249.

cases on questions of law. The Doc. was naturally very disappointed in the decision, although he felt that the going would be very hard and the most he could hope for was a photo finish.[133]

Chifley consulted with Cabinet on the decision and announced that the Government would appeal the matter to the Privy Council as soon as practicable to do so. The nationalisation plans were slowly slipping away together with Labor's hopes of enacting plank 4(a) of the platform, however this did not stop Labor turning its sights towards pursuing the platform in other policy areas whilst the battle for the banks continued.

---

[133] Crisp, 1977, <u>op cit.</u>, p.336.

6 CONSTITUTION ALTERATION INITIATIVES, RENTS AND PRICES, TARIFFS, HOUSING AND SHIPPING

The nationalisation of the Banks was the focus of everybody's attention but in April 1948 the Government moved to enact the Customs Tariff legislation in line with plank 6 in the Methods Section of the platform that called on Labor to introduce legislation to provide 'Additional tariff preferences to the United Kingdom or other countries, conditional upon equitable reciprocal arrangements' and Labor passed a number of Acts to legislate plank 6 of the platform into law, including the Customs Tariff (Canadian Preference) Act 1948; the Customs Tariff (Canadian Preference No.2) Act 1948; the Customs Tariff (Canadian Preference No.3) Act 1948; the Customs Tariff (New Zealand Preference) Act 1948; the Customs Tariff (New Zealand Preference No.2) Act 1948 and the Customs Tariff (Southern Rhodesia Preference) Act 1948. The Acts were passed through the Parliament with minimal debate and with no controversy compared with other legislation. In fact, at the end of May 1948 the people of Australia went to the polls and voted in a referendum on Rents and Prices and compared to the publicity and furore directed at the Banking legislation, the referendum was almost a non-event.

<u>Constitution Alteration Initiative - The Rents and Prices Referendum</u>

The Referendum was also in line with plank 3 on the 'Economic' section of the platform that called for 'Price Control',[134] that was adopted by Conference in September 1948. The Price and Rents referendum was a core Labor policy and the Party had pursued the issue in two previous, unsuccessful, referendum campaigns in 1944 and 1946. The Government had been reliant on the defence power to regulate prices and rents, however it had been nearly three years since the end of WWII and viability of the Government maintaining control via the defence power, in peacetime, was diminishing. On 19 November 1947, Holloway the Minister for Labor and National Service outlined Labor's plan to implement plank 3 of the 'Economic' section of the platform that called for 'Price Control' with the introduction of the Constitution Alteration (Rents and Prices) Bill 1947:

> To safeguard the Australian People from inflation and depression, and to keep in check the profiteer and the racketeer [that] are nationwide problems ... The object of the Bill is to give permanent, nationwide protection to every tenant, every income earner, every housewife, anxious about what her weekly budget will buy, to every user of services and, indeed, to every purchaser as well as to primary producers dependent on unsheltered markets.

> ... A vital duty of national government is to give its people

---

[134] Australian Labor Party, <u>Official Report of Proceedings of the 18th Commonwealth Triennial Conference</u>, Canberra, 27 September 1948, p.55.

freedom from fear and want which was held out to them in the Atlantic Charter as one of the aims which made the sacrifices of the war worthwhile. I will show that the power to control rents and prices is a power without which the Australian Parliament will be severely handicapped in carrying out this duty in the economic sphere. The Australian Government is therefore convinced that the people should be given the opportunity to arm themselves through their Parliament, with essential power.[135]

Labor's approach to protecting Australians from inflation and depression was not shared by the Opposition who launched another frontal assault on the proposal with Menzies outlining the tenor of the future referendum campaign stating:

When these proposed powers are added to the bank monopoly now created, the result will be, in the central government, an enormous power to control all industry – to control it through the instrument of the banking monopoly and through powers of the kind to which I have just briefly referred ... if this Bill were to pass and this referendum were to succeed, what would happen would represent the perfect state of affairs for the central planner, who is, after all, the vital element in the socialist, or, as I would prefer to call it, the servile state.

... We believe that the immediate battle is not between control or no control, but between temporary control and permanent control. Finally, we believe that the ultimate battle is between the basic democratic conception of a free community and the socialist conception of a community which takes its orders from the central authority and enjoys only such freedom as its masters permit.[136]

---

[135] *C.P.D.*, Vol. 195, 19 November 1947, p.2306.

The 'socialist' bogey had been raised again, however the Bill passed through the Parliament and on 29 April 1948 Caucus discussed the pending Referendum proposal and 'Dr Evatt circulated amongst members a statement in reference to Price Control and the States'.[137] Chifley addressed Caucus on the forthcoming campaign, the Caucus minutes noted:

> The Prime Minister stated that the general organisation of the Prices Referendum Campaign was well in hand in all States and that the States had selected their campaign directors and the commonwealth Government was co-operating with them in the campaign.[138]

Chifley's last formal address to his Caucus colleagues may have been positive and upbeat, however on 29 May 1948, the referendum proposal was presented to the Australian people who dealt it a savage blow, with only 40.66% of voters supporting it. The vote was significant in that, out of the twenty-two referenda proposals that had been put to the country since Federation it was the second vote in history that was not supported by a single state[139] and with a total vote of 40.66% it was the third lowest supported initiative since 1901.[140] The referendum result was a blow to Labor together with its ability to enact policy planks in the Platform, although the result should not have come as a surprise given the anti-Labor sentiment that had been whipped up in the community over the nationalisation of the banks. Chifley provided

---

[136] *C.P.D.*, Vol. 195, 27 November 1947, pp.2831-38.

[137] *Caucus Minutes*, 29 April 1947.

[138] ibid.

[139] On 6 March 1927 Bruce proposed the Marketing without restriction of section 92 regarding interstate trade.

[140] On 26 April 1911, Fisher introduced the Legislative Powers: trade and commerce; labour; combinations and monopolies referenda that only received 39.42% of the vote. Also, On 6 March 1927 Bruce proposed the Marketing without restriction of section 92 regarding interstate trade that only received 36.26%.

a simple overview of what he regarded as the reason for the defeat:

> Over £100,000 was spent at the prices referendum and a
> lot of Labor people were misled and voted 'No'.[141]

Chifley's analysis was not shared by the press, however the
Melbourne *Age* was surprisingly balanced in its review of the
referendum defeat:

> Saturday's vote must be regarded as a heavy reverse for the
> Chifley Government and the Federal Labor Party. Unlike
> many previous referenda, each State returned the same
> decisive answer: the only variation seems to have been in
> degree of emphasis. Seldom, if ever, was a proposal so
> firmly and unequivocally rejected in the proper democratic
> process …
>
> The rebuff could have been avoided if the Government had
> heeded the disinterested advice of those who warned
> months ago of the risks of making a third request, after two
> other attempts - that of 1944 and that of 1946 - had failed
> …
>
> It is clear that masses of people who put Labor into office,
> and twice renewed its tenure, seized the opportunity to
> declare that they did not want the system of controls,
> restraints and restrictions grafted on the country's
> peacetime life.[142]

Commonwealth Housing Scheme

---

[141] Australian Labor Party, <u>Official Report of Proceedings of the 18th
Commonwealth Triennial Conference</u>, Melbourne, 30 September 1948, pp.49-
50.
[142] *Age*, Melbourne, 31 May 1948.

The referendum result did not dampen Chifley or Labor's pursuit of the platform. On 8 September 1948, Labor introduced the Loan (Housing) Bill to strengthen plank 17 of the Social Reform section of the platform providing for Labor to establish and maintain an 'Adequate Housing Scheme':

> The purpose of the Bill is to obtain parliamentary approval for further advances to the states of capital funds totalling £14,000,000 in accordance with the provisions of the *Commonwealth and State Housing Agreement Act* 1945.[143]

The legislation consolidated the housing scheme in line with the platform and the positive impact of the scheme was highlighted in the Commonwealth Official Yearbook:

> From the inception of the Commonwealth and State Housing Agreement in April, 1944 to 30th June, 1948, the five States operating under agreement had completed 15,271 dwellings. A further 10.900 dwellings were under construction at that date. In the period mentioned, the Commonwealth advanced £31,115,000 to the States to finance the acquisition and development of land and the construction of dwellings.[144]

Labor's commitment to strengthening core social policy planks was commendable and it also continued to pursue strengthening Australia's public health system in line with section 4(d) of the Methods section of the platform that sought the 'nationalisation of public health', with the introduction of legislation to combat the growing incidence in Australia of tuberculosis. Although, the legislation did not seek to nationalise the health system, it was an

---

[143] *C.P.D.*, Vol. 198, 8 September 1948, pp.274-5.
[144] *The Official Year Book of the Commonwealth of Australia*, 1946-1947, No. 37, p.1201.

important national measure that strengthened the Government's continuing pursuit of the plank. The incidence of Tuberculosis in the Australian community was a matter of major significance and a coordinated national response was required to combat it. On 30 September Holloway, Minister for Labour and National Service, introduced the Tuberculosis Bill into the House that sought to address the problem:

> One of the greatest tasks confronting the nation at this time is the maintenance of national health … One of the greatest victories which we could achieve in this country would be to destroy or reduce, by combined action, the scourge of tuberculosis. This disease is as much the enemy of our people as is any military force which confronted us in the recent war.

> The campaign against tuberculosis authorised by this measure is an example of Commonwealth-State cooperation and collaboration at its best, working on a uniform plan for the positive health of the people.[145]

The Tuberculosis legislation was important to the Government's commitment to providing a viable national health service and it was a precursor to the introduction of the National Health Service Bill. On 24 November Senator McKenna outlined the Bill to the chamber:

> The Bill which it is my privilege to introduce stems from the Government's belief that, apart from spiritual considerations, the health of the people is the foundation upon which all their happiness and all their powers as a nation are built. The Bill … introduces the national health service as a further step to improve the lot of the Australian

---

[145] *C.P.D.*, Vol. 198, 30 September 1948, pp.1066-68.

people and as a direct attack on disease and sickness and their aftermaths, misery and want.[146]

The legislation strengthened Labor's commitment to providing a strong public health system and it was not drafted to nationalise the system, primarily because the high Court had made a point of striking down legislation that vaguely resembled the nationalisation of the system, a point Senator McKenna highlighted during debate:

> Before the amendment, late in 1946, of section 51 of the Commonwealth Constitution, this Parliament was very greatly restricted in its power to deal with problems affecting the health of the people of Australia ... The Government does not contemplate, nor in fact does the constitutional amendment it recently sought and obtained permit, any nationalisation of doctors, dentists or members of allied professions and occupations.[147]

In fact the chances of Labor actually nationalising or socialising any industry or group, especially in the area of health, was made almost impossible by the restrictive judgements of the High Court in related matters.[148]

Commonwealth Shipping Line

The judicial impediments faced by Labor did not stop it pursuing the platform and in December 1948 the Government introduced legislation to revitalise Australia's shipping industry in line with the following three planks of the platform:

---

[146] *C.P.D.*, Vol. 200, 24 November 1948, p.3372.
[147] ibid., pp.3373-4.
[148] see; *Attorney General (Victoria) & ors. v Commonwealth* (October-November 1945) 71 C.L.R. 237; and *British Medical Association v Commonwealth* (August-October 1949) 79 C.L.R. 201

<u>Shipping</u>

1.   Accelerated shipbuilding program to the maximum capacity of Australian ship yards, to overcome shipping shortages.

2.   The maintenance of adequate shipping facilities to meet Interstate requirements and the special difficulties of Tasmania, Western Australia and the Northern Territory.[149]

<u>Rural</u>

5.   The institution of a Commonwealth Shipping service for the carriage of products, both interstate and overseas.[150]

On 9 December Senator Ashley, Minister for Shipping, introduced the Shipping Bill into the Parliament to enact the above planks:

> In introducing this Bill, I should like to assure the members of the Opposition, in anticipation of their usual protests in regard to socialisation, that there is no provision in the Bill for the nationalisation of the shipping industry. The objectives of the Government in introducing the Bill are, first, to provide for the maintenance of the Australian mercantile marine, secondly, to provide for the maintenance of the shipbuilding industry in Australia, and, thirdly, to provide for the establishment of a Commonwealth line of steamers ...

> This Bill will provide the measures needed for the

---

[149] Australian Labor Party, <u>Official Report of Proceedings of the 18th Commonwealth Triennial Conference</u>, Canberra, 27 September 1948, p.55.
[150] <u>ibid</u>., p.57.

maintenance and development, on sound lines, of the Australian shipping and shipbuilding industries. Experience has fully demonstrated that the fostering of these industries is necessary, first, from the point of view of the defence of Australia, and secondly, to ensure that those industries shall continue as sound and prosperous parts of the Australian industrial economy.[151]

Labor passed the Shipping legislation and again enacted key planks in the platform, however the success of the *Shipping Act* 1949 was the last substantive plank of the platform enacted by the Government before the federal election in December. Also, domestic legislative developments were eclipsed by developments on the New South Wales coal fields and the Privy Council in London where the Council was hearing the *Bank Nationalisation Case*. The Privy Council heard the appeal from 14 March to 1 June and again the judgement was not favourable to Labor.[152] Chifley studied the judgement and declared that, 'bank nationalisation was perforce a dead issue'.[153] On 31 July 1949, David Berry of the Brisbane *Sunday Mail* wrote:

> The decision of the Privy Council against the nationalisation of banking in Australia touched off an all-out campaign by the banks and by bank officers to sink Chifley at the federal elections towards the end of this year.[154]

In October 1949, Chifley addressed Labor's Federal Executive and told them that, 'We definitely will not do anything that is outside the Constitution'.[155] A year after his defeat at the 1949 federal elections Chifley spoke about the nationalisation clause in Labor's

---

[151] *C.P.D.*, Vol. 200, 9 December 1948, pp.4218-4225.
[152] see; *Commonwealth v Bank of New South Wales* (1949) [1950] A.C. 235.
[153] Crisp, 1977, op cit., p.338.
[154] *Sunday Mail* (Brisbane), 31 July 1949; as cited in Crisp, 1977, op cit., p.339.
[155] ibid., p.338.

platform stating:

> The plank of the Labor Party's Platform regarding socialisation is being used by our opponents to create fears ... It has to be remembered that the Commonwealth Parliament's constitutional power is limited. It is not the objective of the Labor Party to go around socialising everything.[156]

Labor's drive to nationalise the banks had been clearly thwarted by the Constitution and the interpretative disposition of the judiciary, who were, in respect of this issue, the major impediments to Labor enacting plank 4(a) of the platform. Labor's woes were further compounded by events on the coal fields of New South Wales where communist influence in the mines had led to a massive strike that virtually crippled industry from June to August 1949. In response to the strike Chifley enacted the *National Emergency (Coal Strike) Act* 1949 that made it an offence for trade unions and their members to provide financial assistance to support the strike. In the middle of the Coal strike Chifley addressed the New South Wales Branch of the party and outlined his vision for the future:

> I have had the privilege of leading the Labor Party for nearly four years ... No Labor Minister or leader ever has an easy job ... But the strength of the movement cannot come from us. We may make plans and pass legislation to help and direct the economy of the country. But the job of getting the things the people of the country want comes from the roots of the Labour movement – the people who support it ... I try to think of the Labour movement, not as putting an extra sixpence into somebody's pocket, or making somebody Prime Minister or Premier, but as a

---

[156] Stargaardt, A.W., <u>Things Worth Fighting For: Speeches by Joseph Benedict Chifley.</u> Melbourne University Press, Australia, 1952, p.71.

movement bringing something better to the people, better standards of living, greater happiness to the mass of the people. We have a great objective – the light on the hill – which we aim to reach by working for the betterment of mankind not only here but anywhere we may give a helping hand.[157]

Chifley's famous 'light on the hill' speech galvanised Labor and provided it with a clear focus for the forthcoming election. The Government had been in office since 1941, with Chifley as Prime Minister since Curtin's death in April 1945. The achievements of the Chifley Government were impressive, since 1946 it had:

> … passed more acts and more significant legislation than had been enacted in any other national parliament.[158]

An impressive summation of the Government's achievements in enacting key planks of the platform in relation to health, social services and economy in general was provided by Senator McKenna during debate on the National Health Service Bill when he stated:

> The Commonwealth Government, under agreement with the States, has legislated to provide adequate housing for families in the lower ranges of income. It has interested itself actively in the fields of preventative medicine and research, nutrition, child health and industrial hygiene. During its term of office, as a part of its approach to community welfare, the Government has doubled the amount of child endowment payments, trebled maternity benefits, and doubled the rate of invalid and age pensions. It has introduced widows' pensions and unemployment and

---

[157] ibid., p.107.
[158] McMullin, 1991, op cit., p.253.

sickness benefits. In furtherance of its policy to overcome the economic hazards of ill health, the Government has provided public hospital benefits, private hospital benefits, and pharmaceutical benefits and is about to introduce a measure to authorise an agreement with the states to relieve patients in mental hospitals and their relatives from the obligation of contributing to the maintenance of those patients. The Government has, in cooperation with the States, initiated a nationwide attack on the scourge of tuberculosis. It has sponsored improved conditions of work and has vigorously pursued a policy of full employment.[159]

The Government had brought the country through the second world war. It had legislated during war and in the peace and maintained an impressive list of achievements. Even with the bank nationalisation propaganda and the issue of Communism and Communists in Australia, and in the party, Labor would still enter the election with a favourable list of credits. Chifley called the election for 10 December 1949 and in the ensuing campaign Labor was soundly defeated. Four Ministers, Dedman, Scully, Barnard and Lemmon lost their seats along with seven backbenchers. The *Commonwealth Electoral Act* 1948 had enlarged the House from seventy-five to one hundred and twenty-one members of which Labor only won forty-seven and the Liberal and Country Party's securing no fewer than seventy-four seats an increase of forty-five seats since the 1946 poll.[160]

The loss signalled an end to Labor's plans for continued post-war reconstruction initiatives and although the pursuit of policy planks

---

[159] *C.P.D.*, Vol. 200, 24 November 1948, p.3373.

[160] The Act increased representation in the House and changed the voting system in the Senate from a winner takes all to a system based on proportional representation. The Act was in direct conflict with plank 3(e) of the 'Methods' section of the platform that specifically called for the abolition of the Senate: the Act actually strengthened it.

such as the nationalisation of the Banks had impacted on the party's electoral viability, Chifley was unperturbed. Chifley believed in the Labor Party and the wider labour movement and viewed it as a vehicle to ameliorate the lot of the worker:

> Labor, as I understand it, is a party of reform. Labor is not a party that stands for the retention of the *status quo*. The Labor Party, in defeat or victory, must fight for what it believes to be right, whether that brings electoral success or not.[161]

Chifley's defeat was highlighted by McMullin who cited a 'throwaway line' by Chifley as to his demise:

> ... afterwards Chifley wryly quipped that his government fell because people who could not afford a bus ticket when Labor came to office were now up in arms about petrol rationing.[162]

Chifley's own local newspaper agreed with his bus fare analogy:

> Never before has the Commonwealth been so prosperous and never before have its people been more prosperous as they are today ... Saturday's vote proved a striking illustration of both the fickleness and frailties of human nature ... Hundreds of illustrations can be given to show that men who, when they were struggling for existence were enthusiastic supporters of Labor. However, like the horse who is docile and tractable when underfed, and then when he is provided with an abundance of corn, turns and bites the hand which provided it. So it was with altogether too many workers on Saturday.[163]

---

[161] Crisp, 1977, op cit., p.342.
[162] McMullin, 1991, op cit., p.255.
[163] *National Advocate* (Bathurst), 12 December 1949.

The Chifley Government had enacted significant legislation based on the platform that benefited many especially the working classes, however the residual effects of Bank nationalisation, continued petrol rationing and the emergence of the Communist Party in Australia, were all issues that went against Labor.

7 CONCLUSION

Chifley came to office after the death of John Curtin and at a time when Australia and its troops were still fighting in World war II. Curtin's death was a huge blow to Chifley and indeed the entire labour movement, however Chifley moved quickly to fill the considerable void left by his good friend and former leader and he wasted little time in setting Labor on a path of reform to enact the platform. Chifley's government introduced legislation covering all areas of the platform.

The Government tackled the big issues of the time and fought hard to pursue established platform planks. Chifley had a number of successes and some spectacular failures and like Fisher before him, Chifley had shown that a Labor Government, controlling both Houses, during a time of relative stability, could achieve significant reform based on the platform. Also, like Fisher, Chifley experienced the effects of restrictive interpretations of the Constitution by the High Court as well as seeing important referenda initiatives based on key platform planks defeated.

The Chifley government was only the second Labor administration in nearly forty-five years of federation that actually controlled both Houses of Parliament in a period of relative peace and economic stability.[164] The control of the House and Senate is especially important to reforming governments like Labor, for without control of the Senate Labor's legislative program is susceptible to being destroyed in that chamber, as was the case with the Scullin government's legislative program to combat the Depression in the early 1930s. Labor control of the Senate from 1945-1949 played a major part in Chifley's ability to pursue and enact large parts of the platform including legislative initiatives to strengthen the Commonwealth Bank, to provide life insurance, to provide national laws dealing with marriage and divorce, as well as introducing significant measures to rebuild and develop northern Australia in the aftermath of the war. The government also pursued major infrastructure, social welfare and public health policy initiatives including the provision of a comprehensive Commonwealth Housing scheme, the introduction of a standard national rail system, the nationalisation of wireless transmission, together with legislation providing comprehensive hospital benefits and a national tuberculosis treatment scheme.

In 1946 Labor went to the polls and was returned with a comfortable mandate to continue with its program of post-war reconstruction. The Government introduced substantial constitution alteration initiatives to provide it with the power to pursue the platform *en masse* and for the first time in the history of the party they were successful in securing the passage of the Social Services Referendum in 1946. The success of the Social Services

---

[164] Curtin's victory in the 1943 federal poll also provided Labor with control of the Senate, however even though Labor won the poll on 21 August 1943, it had to wait until 1 July 1944 for the new Labor Senator's terms to commence. Also, Curtin's government was elected during the second world war and was still committed to a program of total war.

referendum was tempered somewhat by the fact that referendums on Organised Marketing of Primary Products, Industrial Employment, and Rents and Prices were rejected at the ballot box. However, despite the referendum results Labor continued to pursue and enact key platform planks including the establishment of a Commonwealth Shipping line as well the introduction of comprehensive navigation and shipping laws for Australian merchant vessels. Labor's success at enacting the platform was comparable to the second Fisher government of 1910-1913, however placing the successes to one side, arguably the biggest platform issue to confront Chifley during his time as Prime Minister centred on his ill-fated plans to nationalise Australia's banking industry. Chifley's plan to nationalise the banking sector was a bold initiative to enact a key platform plank that eventually was struck down by successive verdicts of the High Court and the Privy Council.

Chifley's success at implementing the platform, like Fisher before him, demonstrated that a Labor Government controlling both Houses during a time of relative peace and stability could achieve significant reform based on the platform. Also, like Fisher, Chifley experienced the effects of restrictive interpretations of the Constitution by the High Court as well as seeing important referenda initiatives based on key platform planks defeated.

8 BIBLIOGRAPHY

Newspapers, Journals and websites

Bathurst National Advocate

Canberra Times

Medical Journal of Australia

National Advocate (Bathurst)

Newcastle Morning Herald

Sunday Mail (Brisbane)

The Age

Tribune, (Sydney)

Court Cases

City of Melbourne v Commonwealth (State Banking Case) 74 C.L.R. 31.

Australian National Airways Pty Ltd and ors. V Commonwealth (October-November 1945) 71 C.L.R. 29

British Medical Association v Commonwealth (August-October 1949) 79 C.L.R. 201

City of Melbourne v Commonwealth (The State Banking Case) (July-August 1947) 74 C.L.R. 31.

Bank of New South Wales v Commonwealth (February-August 1948) 76 C.L.R. 1

Attorney General (Victoria) & ors. v Commonwealth (October-November 1945) 71 C.L.R. 237; and *British Medical Association v Commonwealth* (August-October 1949) 79 C.L.R. 201

Commonwealth v Bank of New South Wales (1949) [1950] A.C. 235.

<u>Government Publications</u>

C.P.D., Vol. 181, 9 March 1945, p.546-7.

C.P.D., Vol. 181, 21 March 1945, p.752.

C.P.D., Vol. 181, 22 March 1945, p.785.

C.P.D., Vol. 182, 25 May 1945, p.2144.

C.P.D., Vol. 182, 25 May 1945, p.2145-6.

C.P.D., Vol. 183, 4 July 1945, p.4049.

C.P.D., Vol. 183, 18 July 1945, p.4179.

C.P.D., Vol. 184, 25 July 1945, pp.4556-7.

C.P.D., Vol. 184, 27 July 1945, pp.4690-3.

C.P.D., Vol. XC, 17 October 1919, pp.13548-9.

C.P.D., Vol. 184, 20 July 1945, p.4350.

C.P.D., Vol. 184, 1 August 1945, p.4841.

C.P.D., Vol. 184, 12 September 1945, p.5299.

C.P.D., Vol. 184, 13 September 1945, pp.5385-6.

C.P.D., Vol. 185, 3 & 4 October 1945, p.6430.

C.P.D., Vol. 186, 27 March 1946, pp.646-7.

C.P.D., Vol. 186, 27 March 1946, pp.650-1.

C.P.D., Vol. 186, 27 March 1946, pp.651-3.

C.P.D., Vol. 187, 20 June 1946, pp.1653-4.

C.P.D., Vol. 188, 24 July 1946, pp.3007-8.

C.P.D., Vol.187, 2 August 1946, p.3625-6.

C.P.D., Vol. 190, 21 February 1947, p.123.

C.P.D., Vol. 191, 27 March 1947, pp.1266-7.

C.P.D., Vol. 191, 1 May 1947, pp.1791-2.

C.P.D., Vol. 191, 15 May 1947, p.2392.

C.P.D., Vol. 192, 30 May 1947, p.3198.

C.P.D., Vol 192, 4 June 1947, p.3319.

C.P.D., Vol. 193, 15 October 1947, p.796.

C.P.D., Vol. 194, 23 October 1947, pp.1279-83.

C.P.D., Vol. 195, 19 November 1947, p.2306.

C.P.D., Vol. 195, 27 November 1947, pp.2831-38.

C.P.D., Vol. 198, 8 September 1948, pp.274-5.

C.P.D., Vol. 198, 30 September 1948, pp.1066-68.

C.P.D., Vol. 200, 9 December 1948, pp.4218-4225.

C.P.D., Vol. 200, 24 November 1948, p.3373.

C.P.D., Vol. 200, 24 November 1948, p.3372.

The Official Year Book of the Commonwealth of Australia, 1946-1947, No. 37, p.1201.

ALP Federal Conference Records

Australian Labor Party, <u>Official Report of the Sixth Commonwealth Conference of the Australian Labor Party</u>, Adelaide, 4 June 1915.

Australian Labor Party, <u>Official Report of Proceedings of the 15th Commonwealth Conference</u>, Canberra, 5 May 1939.

Australian Labor Party, <u>Official Report of Proceedings of the 16th Commonwealth Conference</u>, Sydney, 16 December 1943.

Australian Labor Party, <u>Official Report of Proceedings of the 17th Commonwealth Triennial Conference</u>, Melbourne, 26-30 November 1945.

Australian Labor Party, <u>Official Report of Proceedings of the 18th Commonwealth Triennial Conference</u>, Canberra, 27 September 1948.

Australian Labor Party, <u>Official Report of Proceedings of the 18th Commonwealth Triennial Conference</u>, Melbourne, 30 September 1948.

Australian Labor Party, <u>Official Report of Proceedings of the 18th Commonwealth Triennial Conference</u>, Canberra, 27 September 1948.

ALP Federal Caucus Minutes

Caucus Minutes, 10 May 1945.

Caucus Minutes, 19 February 1945.

Caucus Minutes, 20 February 1945.

Caucus Minutes, 12 March 1946.

Caucus Minutes, 29 April 1947.

Caucus Minutes, 16 September 1947.

Books and Journal Articles

Chifley, B., (1952) <u>Things Worth Fighting For: Speeches by Joseph Benedict Chifley</u>. Melbourne University Press.

Crisp, L.F., (1961) <u>Ben Chifley: A Political Biography</u>. Angus and Robertson Publishers, Melbourne, Australia.

Crisp, L.F., (1977) <u>Australian National Government</u>. Longman Cheshire, Melbourne, Australia.

Day, D., (1999) <u>John Curtin: a Life</u>. Harper Collins Publishers, Pty, Australia.

Duthie, G., (1984) <u>I Had 50,000 Bosses: Memoirs of a Labor Backbencher 1946-1975.</u>. Angus & Robertson, Sydney.

Haylen, L., (1969) <u>Twenty Years Hard Labor.</u> McMillan & Co. Pty. Ltd. Melbourne, Australia.

Hayward, D., (1996) <u>The Reluctant Landlords? A history of Public Housing in Australia.</u>   see: <u>http://www.infoxchange.net.au/rhchome/iurhc/index.htm</u>

Kelly, V., (1971) <u>A Man of the People</u>. Alpha, Sydney, 1971.

McMullin, R., (1991) <u>The Light on the Hill: The Australian Labor Party 1891-1991</u>. Oxford University Press, Australia.

Sawer, G., (1963) <u>Australian Federal Politics and Law 1929-1949</u>. Melbourne University Press, Australia.

Stargaardt, A.W., (1952) <u>Things Worth Fighting For: Speeches by Joseph Benedict Chifley.</u> Melbourne University Press, Australia.

Cablegram D769 LONDON, 7 May 1945, 10.19 a.m. [AA:A1066, H45/1013/2/2/2] located at:

http://www.info.dfat.gov.au/info/historical/HistDocs.nsf/vVolume/AA8726EO249A0F8I

ABOUT THE AUTHOR

Dr John McSwiney holds degrees in Economics/Politics and Law, he has a Masters of Politics and a Doctorate of Philosophy from Monash University. John joined the Labor Party when he was 18 and won preselection for the Federal seat of Isaacs when he was 24 contesting the seat as part of Paul Keating's team at the 1993 Federal election. John has had careers in politics, law, government and international business. His roles have included being a Barrister and Solicitor of the Supreme Court of Victoria; the Director International Education, VCAA; CEO Haileybury International School, China; and Director, Technical Training (Eng.) Royal Australian Navy.

Chifley and Australian Post War Reconstruction

99